THE GREAT PRINCIPLE OF THE TORAH

Examining Seven Talmudic Claims to the Defining Principles of Judaism

RABBI JACK BIELER

KODESH PRESS

The Great Principle of the Torah:
Examining Seven Talmudic Claims to the Defining
Principles of Judaism
© Jack Bieler 2016

ISBN: 978-1-947857-21-6
Hardcover Edition

All rights reserved. Except for brief quotations in printed reviews, no part of this publication may be reproduced, stored in a retrieval system, or transmitted in any form or by any means (printed, written, photocopied, visual electronic, audio, or otherwise) without the prior permissions of the publisher.

Biblical translations are based on the JPS translation available at mechon-mamre.org, and translations of the Talmud are based on the Soncino edition available at e-daf.com. Both are in the public domain.

Originally published February 2016.
Present text has been slightly updated, July 2016.

The publisher extends its gratitude to
Rabbi Yeshayahu Ginsburg for proofreading,

Published & Distributed by
Kodesh Press L.L.C.
New York, NY
www.KodeshPress.com
kodeshpress@gmail.com

To Joan

All that is mine is hers

Table of Contents

Introduction 9

1. Hillel's "Entire Torah" and R. Akiva's "Great Principle" . 15
2. Ben Azzai's Central Principle 45
3. Paring the Torah's Principles 74
4. In All Your Ways Know Him 115
5. Pleasantness and Peace 148
6. Lovingkindness 187
7. Lawfulness 212

Conclusion 256
Appendix 259

Introduction

I have long been concerned with trying to establish for myself as well as my students and congregants what the point of Judaism was. Throughout my forty-year career in Jewish education and the rabbinate, I have been continually amazed at how little serious and prolonged reflection was devoted to making sense of the goals of Jewish tradition and literature. I have found this to be true not only for Jews who have chosen not to place Judaism at the center of their lives, but also those who ostensibly devote their lives to personally enacting their religious heritage as fully as possible. This book is an attempt to articulate, using Jewish primary and secondary sources, one rabbi's view of what the essential values are that comprise the ideal Jewish lifestyle. My intent is to catalyze thought and conversation about these "meta-values," concepts that stand alone as goals and ideals towards which the spiritual individual ought to strive and realize within one's own life.

Many years ago, I found myself forced by circumstance to begin to think about what those values should be. In 1974, I completed my studies for rabbinical ordination and began to teach in a Modern Orthodox high school. I was immediately confronted with a dilemma that I found deeply challenging. A financial scandal was headline news, and for several weeks, the principle figures in the sensationalist trial were observant Jews. I realized that attempting to teach Jewish tradition to adolescents, no small task in its own right, would now become that much more difficult, since my students could not help but wonder about the effectiveness and relevance of a religious system that seemed to allow for high-profile Orthodox adults to engage in such inconsistency and immorality.[1] At the time, I chose to emphasize that a distinction must be made between the religious system that is manifest in our primary sources and communal traditions, on the one hand, and how particular individuals process and enact that tradition, on the other. Regrettably, it is a distinction that I have found myself invoking many times during my rabbinic career. Not only did I have to remind myself of this unsavory dichotomy in order to address frequent questions posed by my students and congregants, but also to deal with similar concerns arising in my own mind.

Furthermore, my experience in education and communal work has taught me that a virtually infinite number of variables play important roles in the nature and quality of our religious observances and moral standards. These variables include psychological, developmental, sociological, political, educational, and professional factors, which naturally evolve during our lives. I have often commented that we are all works-in-progress with regard to the development of personal ideals and perspectives, including our religious outlook and commitment, as well as overall moral sensibilities. And it must be said that while the term "progress" as applied to the course of human life might be inherently positive, the path entailed in making progress in matters of belief, as well as in moral and ethical standards, is often

Introduction

full of ups and downs, advances and retreats. Therefore, in order to maintain a sense our ultimate goals in such an endeavor, I would like to attempt to define as clearly as possible what it is that all of us should be striving to achieve.

It is my contention that a key cognitive factor as to why the behaviors and beliefs comprising a traditional Jewish lifestyle sometimes fail to serve as either a stopgap or corrective for improper behavior, is that many of us struggle with the fundamental "forest-and-tree" problem. On the one hand, the myriad finite practices imposed by Jewish halakhic observance might actually serve to obfuscate the specific goals of such a lifestyle. On the other hand, our primary sources of Jewish tradition—the Tanakh, the Talmud and its commentaries, Midrash, the codes, and responsa literature—are so dense, ambiguous, massive, and at times even contradictory, that they pose an intractable difficulty in determining what the point of all of this material is, even for the devoted student of Torah. As a result many Jews, even knowledgeable ones, are confused, overwhelmed, or avoid reflecting about the complexities of life and religion. We all too often lack the requisite perspective that establishes parameters of Jewish moral and spiritual observance, or are simply unable to pay attention to and vigorously follow through on the overall goal or goals of Judaism. It is to be expected that differences of opinion about the ultimate purpose of Jewish observance are found in our primary sources and have been articulated by major figures in Jewish tradition.

I believe that this book's contribution is to help observant individuals realize Jewish values by means of clarifying the ideas underlying our religious literature and legal codes by identifying and analyzing the meta-principles of Judaism. I do not wish at all to suggest that adherence to such values can replace careful and thorough engagement with the Torah's commandments; I only wish to augment and clarify acts of observance with a developed awareness of the purposes of this lifestyle—the desired effects upon those who follow it. Hopefully, the contents of these pages will not only help clarify the specific purposes of committing to living a comprehensively observant life within a Jewish framework, but also provide a baseline by which individuals can measure where they currently stand and which areas and directions they might consider for future personal development.

Methodologically, the meta-principles that I have chosen to analyze are global statements by rabbinic authorities who suggest that a particular idea or concept is central to the entire Torah enterprise. When someone states categorically, or implies, "This is the central goal of Judaism," or, "The Torah's commandments are manifestations of this principle," I will attempt to define the concept, test its veracity with respect to Torah as a whole, suggest reasons behind why this individual was drawn to the proposed idea, and speculate how the rule ought to impact on our present-day Jewish experience.[2] While the Talmud contains myriad voices, which often dispute one another, nevertheless, when someone who is authoritative enough to have been included in the official corpus of a rabbinic text offers one of these comprehensive opinions, we should take serious notice, and look to incorporate that view into our own *weltanschauung*. This is the spirit of the talmudic principle *eilu ve-eilu divrei Elokim chaim*, "these and these are the words of the living God."[3] Sources reflecting fundamental disagreements about the essence of Judaism will be of particular interest.

Introduction

The principles that will be defined and discussed are:

- Chapter 1: Hillel's opinion: "What is hateful to you, do not to your neighbor" (*Shabbat* 31a); Rabbi Akiva's opinion: "And you shall love your neighbor as yourself" (Jerusalem Talmud *Nedarim* 9:4).
- Chapter 2: Ben Azzai's opinion: "This is the book of the generations of man in the day that God created man, in the likeness of God made He him" (JT *Nedarim* 9:4).
- Chapter 3: An anonymous opinion in the Talmud which says Habakkuk reduced all the principles of the Torah to one verse, "But the righteous shall live by his faith" (*Makkot* 23b-24a).
- Chapter 4: Bar Kappara's opinion: "In all your ways know Him and He will direct your paths" (*Berakhot* 63a).
- Chapter 5: R. Joseph's opinion: "Her ways are ways of pleasantness and all her paths are peace" (*Gittin* 59a-b).
- Chapter 6: R. Yehudah's opinion: "Anyone who denies the priority of acts of kindness, it is as if he has been *kofer be-ikkar* [denied the most fundamental principle]" (*Kohelet Rabbah* 7:4).
- Chapter 7: R. Elazar's opinion: "The entire Torah is based upon justice" (*Exodus Rabbah* 30:19).

I do not contend that this inventory of principles is exhaustive, and I welcome readers' suggestions to amend and expand the list so that the goals of Jewish observance can become ever clearer still.

Let the conversation begin!

Endnotes

1. I have written in "Three Models to Inspire the Objectives of Torah Instruction in the Modern Orthodox Day School" that day school students should be approached religiously as if they were prospective converts. Since they are potentially dealing with identity crises and deciding how they will live their lives, instruction in Jewish studies should be informed by the choices that they will be making for themselves. (As of the publication of this book, the article is available here: https://rayanotyaakov.files.wordpress.com/2013/10/1993-three-models-to-inspire-the-objectives-of-torah-instruction-in-the-modern-orthodox-day-school.pdf)

2. While I have been independently thinking about this book and its contents for many years, I wish to acknowledge a work that could be considered loosely parallel that was published a few years ago, directed at parents who wish to instill proper Jewish ethics and values within their children: Stanley H. Fischman, *Seven Steps to "Mentschhood": How to Help your Child Become a Mentsch—An Interactive Guide for Parents* (Jerusalem: Penina Press, 2012). I reviewed this book in *Jewish Action*, June 13, 2012. While Mr. Fischman's volume identifies particular Jewish themes and then offers many practical, concrete suggestions for how to help children internalize these ideas, my book is directed at adults, focusing upon the statements of rabbinic sages in the primary sources of our literature, and attempting to raise adult consciousnesses regarding their importance and relevance by means of analysis and reflection.

3. See, e.g., *Eruvin* 13b; *Gittin* 6b.

Chapter 1

Hillel's "Entire Torah" and R. Akiva's "Great Principle"

תלמוד בבלי מסכת שבת דף לא עמוד א
שוב מעשה בנכרי אחד שבא לפני שמאי, אמר לו: גיירני על מנת שתלמדני כל התורה כולה כשאני עומד על רגל אחת. דחפו באמת הבניין שבידו. בא לפני הלל, גייריה. אמר לו: דעלך סני לחברך לא תעביד - היא כל התורה כולה, ואידך - פירושה הוא, זיל גמור.

Babylonian Talmud *Shabbat* **31a**
It happened that a certain non-Jew came before Shammai and said to him, "Convert me on condition that you teach me the whole Torah while I stand on one foot." Thereupon he repulsed him with the builder's cubit which was in his hand. When he went before Hillel, he said to him, "What is hateful to you, do not to your neighbor. That is the entire Torah [*kol ha-Torah kullah*], while the rest is the commentary. Go and learn it."

The Great Principle of the Torah

תלמוד ירושלמי (וילנא) מסכת נדרים פרק ט

[ויקרא יט יח] "ואהבת לרעך כמוך". רבי עקיבה אומר זהו כלל גדול בתורה.

Jerusalem Talmud *Nedarim* 9:4

"You shall love your neighbor as yourself" (Lev. 19:18). R. Akiva says, "This is the central principle [*kelal gadol*] of the Torah."

Hillel's "Entire Torah"

Hillel (110 BCE-10 CE) gives a famous response to a potential convert requesting the Torah be reduced into as few statements as possible. His response is, "What is hateful to you, do not to your neighbor. That is the entire Torah [*kol ha-Torah kullah*], while the rest is the commentary. Go and learn it." This has been called the Silver Rule, whose converse is the Golden Rule and expressed in the affirmative, "Do unto others as you would have others do unto you."

Implicit in the Talmud's account is that Hillel would not have reflected on what he thought was the point of Judaism, had he not been asked this question by the prospective convert. It is possible that defining the key principle of the commandments may not have personally been a priority for Hillel. Perhaps living a traditional Jewish lifestyle in and of itself was deeply meaningful to him, and it is possible that he never before had engaged in reflection and introspection with respect to Judaism as a whole.[1] The Talmud's narrative asserts that what precipitated Hillel's thinking about this issue was the question presented by an outsider. This individual was concerned that converting may prove too onerous or confusing due to the massive amount of material that would be necessary for him to master and observe. Hence even though Hillel was a great scholar, when confronted by this question, he himself may have benefited tremendously from the exchange. By offering an elegant simplification of Judaism, Hillel assisted the potential convert to understand the goal of Judaism, and thereby clarified for him the point of what lay ahead should he choose to become a Jew. Hillel's response is memorialized in the Talmud, making his perspective available to all inquiring minds, even Jews from birth.

Jay Lefkowitz, in his article, "The Rise of Social Orthodoxy: A Personal Account" (*Commentary* 2014) describes a contemporary trend among some observant adherents of Judaism. These are Jews who are committed to the continuity of the Jewish people, Zionists who are deeply devoted to the survival of Israel as a country, who learn regularly from the Torah and religious books, who attend synagogue regularly and keep many of the traditional Jewish practices well, if not perfectly, like Shabbat and *kashrut*. However, many of these Jews are agnostics, and they do not spend much time on theology or developing a system of Jewish beliefs or a philosophical explanation of the commandments. Lefkowitz relates that he could not answer the simple question, "Why do you keep kosher?"

Marianne Novak, in her response "The Rise of 'Social Orthodoxy' Ain't Nothin' New" (*Times of Israel*, April 13, 2014), explains that her father was a Conservative rabbi in Norfolk, Virginia, and growing up as the only Sabbath-observant girl in her town, she was constantly forced to explain Jewish practices to her friends and teachers. When she moved to Far Rockaway, which had a strong Orthodox presence, she realized her peers had never been forced to explain their practice or level of observance, or to test their commitment to Judaism. She was fourteen, and she felt that the Orthodox students looked down on her, even though she had worked much harder to keep her Jewish traditions, and may have even had a more developed theology. Novak argues that it is important for observant Jews to take ownership of their religion by thinking deeply about it and understanding what it signifies regarding God and His service. Otherwise, their commitment could easily be disrupted, if not completely abandoned, under challenging conditions.

It is interesting to consider that Hillel himself may never have been forced to take ownership of his religion in the way Novak describes. While other anecdotes and sayings about and by Hillel demonstrate his deep commitment to the Torah and its commandments (see, e.g., *Yoma* 35b, *Avot* 1:13), nevertheless Hillel may have never seriously contemplated how to express laconically the singular point of the lifestyle to which he was obviously so deeply committed.

Rabbi Eliezer said, *da ma she-tashiv le-apikorus*, "Know what you should respond to a heretic" (*Avot* 2:14). While the simple meaning of this aphorism is that one should attempt to anticipate intellectual challenges that may be posed to you by others, a psychological perspective would insist that the most profound challenges to religion may originate from within one's own mind. In a similar vein, Rabbi Dr. Norman Lamm wrote in his essay "Faith and Doubt" as follows:

> We are naive if we think we can teach Judaism, especially to a young person, without encountering genuine doubt. And the doubts of our contemporaries cannot be silenced by shrill dogmatic assertions or by charming rhetoric, much less by superficial and artificial solutions which fool no one but their creators. Such problems of *emunah* (faith) exist, and we have to meet them forthrightly, whether we like it or not, in our society, among genuinely

committed and observant Jews, in our children—and in our own selves. Indeed, I am more concerned by how we approach doubt that appears in the community of the committed than the doubt that confronts us when we engage in a dialogue with the uncommitted. Anyone who has taught or discussed the fundamentals of Judaism with young Orthodox Jews can testify to the ubiquity of honest doubt, and to the catastrophic consequences of cowardice in dealing with it....[2]

The challenger for whom we should prepare includes ourselves!

From my professional and personal experience, I can provide ample anecdotal evidence that some people born into the Jewish faith, even if they have benefitted from a serious Jewish education and proper observant role models, settle on a different lifestyle. I have wondered to what extent this choice was made, at least in part, as a result of confusion about why all of this ritual and structure is necessary. A central purpose underlying this book is to think about the question posed to Hillel. Its answers may be advantageous not only to outsiders, but to committed Jews as well, whether born into religious families or learning about their faith as adults. Inevitably, every one of us wonders about the same questions sooner or later.

Hillel and *Pirkei Avot*

Hillel's teaching in *Shabbat* 31a should be considered in light of his numerous teachings in *Avot*, including the teaching, "Do not judge a friend until you are in his place" (*Avot* 2:4). Here, the emphasis is on how one even thinks about another person, not merely how he acts towards him. Negative judgments regarding another individual's character or lifestyle can sometimes lead to treating that person improperly, but negative judgment is not the only thing that can lead to maltreatment. For example, a person may lash out at another as the result of excessive self-absorption and indifference, without knowing who gets hurt as a result. Consequently, Hillel's statement to the potential convert appears to be a more basic formula to create an ideal social environment than what is quoted in his name in *Avot*.

Hillel's assertion about judging others appears in a list of his teaching (*Avot* 2:4-7), which contains at least eleven different ideas:

> **4.** Hillel would say: (1) Do not separate yourself from the community. (2) Do not trust in yourself until the day you die. (3) Do not judge your fellow until you have stood in his place. (4) Do not say something that is not readily understood in the belief that it will ultimately be understood [or: Do not say something that ought not to be heard even in the strictest confidence, for ultimately it will be heard]. And (5) do not say, "When I free myself of my concerns, I will study," for perhaps you will never free yourself. **5.** He would also say: (6a) A boor cannot be sin-fearing, (6b) an ignoramus cannot be pious, (6c) a bashful one cannot learn, (6d) a short-tempered person cannot teach, (7) nor does anyone who does much business grow wise. (8) In a place where there are no men, strive to be a man. **6.** (9) He also saw a skull floating upon the water. Said he to it: Because you drowned others, you were drowned; and those who drowned you, will themselves be drowned. **7.** He would also say: (10a) One who increases flesh, increases worms; (10b) one who increases possessions, increases worry; (10c) one who increases wives, increases witchcraft; (10d)

Hillel's "Entire Torah" and R. Akiva's "Great Principle"

one who increases maidservants, increases promiscuity; (10e) one who increases man-servants, increases thievery; (10f) one who increases Torah, increases life; (10g) one who increases study, increases wisdom; (10h) one who increases counsel, increases understanding; (10i) one who increases charity, increases peace. (11a) One who acquires a good name, acquired it for himself; (11b) one who acquires the words of Torah, has acquired life in the World to Come (*Avot* 2:4-7).[3]

Furthermore, his formulation to the potential convert can be compared to six more of Hillel's teachings[4] in *Avot* 1:12-14:

12. ... Hillel would say: (12) Be of the disciples of Aaron—a lover of peace, a pursuer of peace, one who loves the creatures and draws them close to Torah. **13.** He would also say: (13) One who advances his name, destroys his name. (14) One who does not increase, diminishes. (15) One who does not learn is deserving of death. And (16) one who makes personal use of the crown of Torah shall perish. **14.** He would also say: (17a) If I am not for myself, who is for me? (17b) And if I am only for myself, what am I? (17c) And if not now, when?

When we consider the statement in *Shabbat* 31a independently of the quotations in *Avot*, as well as other places throughout the Talmud where Hillel's ideas are recorded, we can form an impression of what Hillel believed was the point of the entire Torah. The multiple ideas attributed to Hillel in *Pirkei Avot* and elsewhere corroborate the sincerity of Hillel's statement to the potential convert that "What is hateful to you, do not to your neighbor. That is the entire Torah [*kol ha-Torah kullah*], while the rest is the commentary. Go and learn it."

Is Hillel's Response a Distortion?

It seems peculiar that Hillel's answer is neither particularly Jewish, nor pointedly spiritual. There is nothing about Jewish distinctiveness, and there is nothing about drawing closer to God. Secular law focuses on the avoidance of hurting others, and exists independently of religious guidance. It is true that religion teaches that people should treat each other equitably, but ideally all people of good will, whether or not they are religious, would avoid inflicting harm, even if that damage does not rise to the level of criminality. The Hippocratic Oath, which is one of the cornerstones of bioethics, demands, "First do no harm." Similarly, John Stuart Mill wrote, "the sole end for which mankind are warranted, individually or collectively, in interfering with the liberty of action of any of their number, is self-protection. That the only purpose for which power can be rightfully exercised over any member of a civilized community, against his will, is to prevent harm to others. His own good, either physical or moral, is not sufficient warrant."[5]

Hippocrates and Mill, among others, develop the idea that avoiding harm is a universal human objective. Yet Hillel seems to say that fair treatment is the dominant or defining trait of Judaism. He invokes the need for empathy, whereby one imagines what it is like to suffer unpleasant human interactions, and uses that sentiment to not perpetrate similar misfortunes upon others. Therefore, when Hillel states that fair treatment is not just one of many religious issues, but the singular objective of Judaism, his words seem counterintuitive. What does Judaism offer that any secular code of conduct does not provide?

Hillel's "Entire Torah" and R. Akiva's "Great Principle"

Hillel's Objective

Hillel emphasized that a Torah community must exercise extraordinary care not to hurt others. He makes this a religious value rather than a pragmatic principle for society, a conclusion which can be understood in light of Maimonides' *Guide for the Perplexed* (2:40). There, Maimonides distinguishes between two types of human leadership:

> It is by no means possible that [man's] society should be perfected except… through a ruler who gauges the actions of the individuals, perfecting that which is deficient and reducing that which is excessive, and who prescribes actions and moral habits that all of them must always practice in the same way, so that the natural diversity is hidden through multiple points of conventional accord and so that the community becomes well-ordered…. It is a part of the wisdom of the Deity… that He put it into its nature that individuals belonging to it should have the faculty of ruling.
>
> Among them there is one to whom the regimen mentioned has been revealed by prophecy directly; he is the prophet…. Among them there are also those who have the faculty to compel people to accomplish, observe, and actualize that which has been established by [him]. [He is] the sovereign who adopts the *nomos* in question….
>
> Accordingly if you find a Law the whole end of which and the whole purpose of the chief thereof, who determined the actions required by it, are directed exclusively toward the ordering of the city and its circumstances and the abolition in it of injustice and oppression… the whole

purpose of that Law being... the arrangement... of the circumstances of people in their relations with one another and provision for their obtaining... a certain something deemed to be *happiness*—you must know that... the man who laid it down belongs to... those who are perfect only in their imaginative faculty [i.e., the *sovereign*].

If on the other hand, you find a Law all of whose ordinances are due to attention being paid... to the soundness of the circumstances pertaining to the body and also the soundness of belief—a Law that takes pains to inculcate correct opinions with regard to God... and with regards to the angels, and that desires to make man wise, to give him understanding, and to awaken his attention, so that he should know the whole of that which exists in its true form—you must know that this guidance comes from Him... and that this Law is Divine....[6]

Maimonides posits that man needs to be among other people to be able to function on the highest level possible. But due to man's manifold natures, some of them extremely caustic to his fellows, it is not possible for him to live among others unless there are regulations which are enforced upon him. Human authorities are responsible for developing the social underpinnings of society. Judaism values that an orderly society be established: "R. Chanina, deputy high priest says: Pray for the welfare of the government, for without fear of it, every person would swallow his fellow alive" (*Avot* 3:2).

However it is left to religious authorities—first the prophets and then the rabbinic leadership—to strive to inspire man to act, not only in accordance with the letter of the divine law, but also adhering to its spirit. Religious law will therefore focus upon the subtle human interactions that might not be societal crimes capable of disrupting civilization per se, but nevertheless are not in accordance with man's intrinsic nature and spiritual potential, nor in the best interests of his fellow man. In light of Maimonides' comments, Hillel is telling the non-Jew that Judaism attempts to extend man's concern for his fellow man beyond merely avoiding criminal activity. Judaism insists that man become sensitive to the totality of the other's soul and spirit.

Nachmanides & the Letter of the Law
Nachmanides captures the essence of how Judaism takes ordinary civil law one step further. He comments on the verse: "And you shall do that which is right and good in the sight of the Lord; that it may be well with you, and that thou may go in and possess the good land which the Lord swore unto your fathers" (Deut. 6:18). Nachmanides writes:

> And our Rabbis suggest a beautiful Midrash concerning this. They say that the verse is referring to compromise and going beyond the letter of the law. And the intention concerning this is that initially God said that one should observe His statutes and His testimonies that He commanded you, and now He says also regarding that which He did not command you, strive to do the good and the right in His eyes, because He loves the good and the right. And this is a great matter, because it is impossible to articulate in the Torah all of the [ideal] behaviors regarding his neighbors and his friends, and all of his interactions [with them] and the improvements that should be made within all societies and states. But once

He mentioned many of them…[7] He now states in general that one should do the good and right in every matter to the point where one should engage in compromise and go beyond the letter of the law… until a person is referred to by others as "wholehearted and righteous."[8]

Like Hillel, when Nachmanides wishes to define what the Rabbis thought was "right and good in the sight of the Lord," in effect the true essence of Judaism, he specifies interpersonal behaviors. According to Nachmanides, religious legislation not only goes further than civil law in guaranteeing appropriate interactions among members of a society within subtle, non-criminal contexts, but the spiritual laws of the Torah should also serve as a baseline for behaviors not specifically addressed or codified as part of Jewish law. Leading a religious lifestyle will therefore guide the observant individual to progressively strive to achieve ever higher levels of sanctity and Godliness.

Hillel's Formula
In matters of worldview, different personalities will be drawn to different aspects of Jewish tradition, and will impart to others their own preferences. Presentations of a worldview should therefore be considered distinct from strict legal (halakhic) discussions. When it comes to practical *halakhah*, objective evaluation is crucial to achieve an accurate and true conclusion. But even when many people observe the same *halakhah*, their religious outlooks regarding the purpose and meaning of these practices may be at considerable variance. This is another application of what King Solomon wrote, "Train up a child in the way he should go, and even when he is old, he will not depart from it" (Proverbs 22:6).

Hillel's "Entire Torah" and R. Akiva's "Great Principle"

I remember Rabbi Joseph B. Soloveitchik making the following point about the Baal Shem Tov and the Vilna Gaon. They both followed the same Torah, but they disagreed with each other, and not improperly, but legitimately in accordance with their different natures.

Additionally, over the course of the generations, practices that were explained in one manner may be explained differently in a later era when sensibilities have changed. For example, Maimonides famously attributed many of the Torah's prohibitions as a response to idolatrous practices (especially in *Guide for the Perplexed*, Part 3). Though this may have satisfied readers in the twelfth century, Jews today are are less likely to accept his interpretations as accurate or relevant. The Torah is eternal and binding in the actions that it commands. However, the Torah rarely delineates the reasons for the commandments, so explicating their purpose is an area where new and relevant interpretations can continuously be developed.

The distinction between matters of perspective (*hashkafah*) and practice (*halakhah*) is highlighted in *Pirkei Avot*. While there is no reason to assume that the Rabbis quoted in *Pirkei Avot* had significant differences in practice, their personal interests and primary concerns may have varied widely in accordance with their natures and learning. These Rabbis are associated with a very limited number of pithy aphorisms. The variety of points of view contained in *Pirkei Avot* is not, in my opinion, meant to determine that one view is more correct than another. Instead, it suggests that each person's attribute or religious sensibility informed his way of looking at the world in a unique way. Granted that when one Rabbi directly confronts another in disagreement, we have no choice other than to account for why they clash. But as long as explicit evidence of such a conflict is absent, we can see the differing positions as articulations of the basic principles that guided these Rabbis' lives, rather than exclusive and conflicting ideologies.

We would rightly expect a wide range of *hashkafot*, in light of the vast variety of personalities that make up the Jewish people. To this effect, the Talmud teaches, "If one sees a crowd of Israelites, he should say: 'Blessed is He who discerneth secrets,' for the mind of each is different from that of the other, just as the face of each is different from that of the other" (*Berakhot* 58a).

In scientific terminology, this is called "hybrid vigor," when the superior qualities of two crossbred species increase the strength of the new life form. Applying it to Israel, this tapestry of differences contributes to the beauty and strength of the nation, provided, of course, that there is mutual respect and understanding.

Rabbi Jonathan Sacks based the title of one of his books, *A Letter in the Scroll*, on a metaphor coined by the Baal Shem Tov that reflects this idea:

> ... the Jewish people is a living Sefer Torah, and every Jew is one of its letters.... A letter on its own has no meaning, yet when letters are joined to others they make a word, words combine with others to make a sentence, sentences connect to make a paragraph, and paragraphs join to make a story.... Every Jew is a letter. Each Jewish family is a word, every community a sentence, and the Jewish people at any one time are a paragraph....[9]

In philosophical matters, it is entirely appropriate to attempt to link a rabbi's personality or history with the worldview that he propounds (as opposed to *halakhah*, which must be analyzed on the merit of the argument alone). Consequently, we can speculate about Hillel's perspective in light of what we are told about his life.

Hillel's "Entire Torah" and R. Akiva's "Great Principle"

There is one event in particular that seems to lead directly to the answer that he gives the potential convert. The Talmud teaches:

> Our Rabbis taught: The poor... come before the [Heavenly] court — They say to the poor: Why have you not occupied yourself with the Torah? If he says: I was poor and worried about my sustenance, they would say to him: Were you poorer than Hillel? It was reported about Hillel the Elder that every day he used to work and earn one *tropaik*, half of which he would give to the guard at the house of learning, the other half being spent for his food and for that of his family. One day he found nothing to earn and the guard at the house of learning would not permit him to enter. He climbed up and sat upon the window to hear the words of the Living God from the mouth of Shemaya and Avtalion. They say that day was the eve of Shabbat in the winter solstice and snow fell down upon him from the sky. When the dawn rose, Shemaya said to Avtalion: "Brother Avtalion, on every day this house is light and today it is dark, is it perhaps a cloudy day?" They looked up and saw the figure of a man in the window. They went up and found him covered by three cubits of snow. They removed him, bathed and anointed him and placed him opposite the fire and they said: "This man deserves that the Shabbat be profaned on his behalf" (*Yoma* 35b).

The account describes an individual so determined to study Torah that he literally risked his life when faced with the possibility of being denied entry to the study hall due to his poverty. No mention is made of an attempt to take his circumstances into consideration, of acknowledging that his exceptional motivation and ability should entitle him to participate and be educated. Hillel could have been offended that he was denied access to the study hall, despite his exceptional abilities, and that might have been disastrous for the Jewish people.

Hillel did not take the approach of Bar Kamtza,[10] and apparently he was not of the opinion that his not receiving special treatment, in the form of free admission to the study hall, reflected a lack of morality and sensitivity by the rabbinic leadership, and by implication, the Torah itself. Nevertheless, the people who guarded entry to the study hall treated him badly. Their behavior could well have influenced him to raise empathy as the highest value in Judaism, especially empathy to someone whose experience might qualitatively be vastly different from one's own.[11]

Rabbi Akiva's Formulation

A few generations after Hillel, Rabbi Akiva (40 CE-137 CE) presented essentially the same principle. The Jerusalem Talmud records the following teaching: "'You shall love your neighbor as yourself' (Lev. 19:18). R. Akiva says, 'This is the central principle [*kelal gadol*] of the Torah'" (Yerushalmi *Nedarim* 9:4).[12] Whereas Hillel's formulation was made in response to a question posed by an outsider, we are not told what led Rabbi Akiva to his conclusion.

The Mishnah discusses a person who has made a formal vow not to derive benefit from a neighbor. After taking that vow, the person comes to regret that decision, and is looking for a means to nullify the formal vow he has made:

> Mishnah: R. Meir also said: A strategy by which it [the vow prohibiting giving benefit to another] can be absolved

> [the process entails going to a scholar and explaining how the vow had been made without realizing certain crucial facts] is based upon what is written in the Torah. And we say to him: Had you known that you were violating, "You shall not take vengeance," "You shall not bear any grudge against the children of your people," or, "You shall love your neighbor as yourself" (all Lev. 19:18), or "...that your brother may live with you" (Lev. 25:36), or that he [the object of the vow] might become poor and you would not be able to provide for him, would you have vowed?
>
> Should he reply, "Had I known that it is so, I would not have vowed," he is absolved.

The Talmud considers the elements contained in this Mishnah. First, by asking a rhetorical question, the Talmud explains why taking revenge or bearing a grudge against another member of the Jewish people is actually self-destructive:

> *Gemara*: It is written, "You shall not take vengeance; you shall not bear any grudge against the children of your people." What constitutes a parable for this? One was cutting something with a knife and accidentally cut his own hand, would he then cut the hand [that had been holding the knife in retaliation]?

The intriguing premise of the *Gemara* is that the Jewish people as a whole should be viewed as a single organism. Consequently, to decide to harm someone who has previously harmed you—whether physically or verbally—is actually compounding the harm that has already adversely affected the original victim![13]

The Great Principle of the Torah

But instead of continuing to explore this evocative perspective that the *Gemara* suggests underlies the first two prohibitions in Lev. 19:18, the discussion takes up the next phrase in the verse that was cited in the Mishnah:

> "You shall love your neighbor as yourself" (Lev. 19:18). R. Akiva says, "This is the central principle [*kelal gadol*] of the Torah."

It would appear that R. Akiva's dramatic evaluation of this mitzvah is neither dependent upon anything previously discussed in the Talmud, nor is it directly pertinent to the Mishnah at hand. Whether or not "You shall love your neighbor as yourself" is a central principle of the Torah, the Mishnah is merely citing the phrase as one of five different phrases, any one of which could be utilized to absolve someone of a vow that he comes to regret.

Hillel's Universalism and Rabbi Akiva's Particularism

Hillel's rule is decidedly universalistic—there is no indication that the words, "What is hateful to you, do not to your neighbor" are directed at a particular segment of humanity. R. Akiva, by citing a biblical verse, particularly one that includes the phrase, "against the children of *your people*" appearing immediately before "You shall love your neighbor as yourself," may understand that this great rule of the Torah applies only to Jews.

In one of his most famous statements, Rabbi Akiva first lauds all of humanity before lauding the status of the Jewish people specifically:

Hillel's "Entire Torah" and R. Akiva's "Great Principle"

He [R. Akiva] also used to say: Beloved is man in that he was created in the image of God. It is a mark of superabundant love that it was made known to him that he had been created in the lmage of God, as it is said, "for in the image of God made He man" (Gen. 9:6).

Beloved are Israel in that they were called children of the All-Present. It was a mark of superabundant love that it was made known to them that they were called children of the All-Present, as it is said, "You are children of the Lord your God" (*Avot* 3:14, quoting Deut. 14:1).

Rabbi Akiva's Lesson Isn't Learned

However, a conundrum regarding another aspect of Rabbi Akiva's life as recorded in the Talmud could explain why he promoted Lev. 19:18 as so central to Judaism, independent of his encounter with the Mishnah in *Nedarim*. In other words, the mere fact that the Mishnah quoted the verse triggered a response from Rabbi Akiva, since that verse had made a deep impression upon him at some point earlier in his life. In a different passage, the Talmud recounts a tragedy that involved a great number of Rabbi Akiva's students:

> It was said that R. Akiva had twelve thousand pairs of disciples, from Gabbatha to Antipatris; and all of them died at the same time because they did not treat each other with respect. The world remained desolate until R. Akiva came to our Masters in the South and taught the Torah to them. These were R. Meir, R. Yehudah, R. Yosi, R. Shimon and R. Elazar ben Shammua; and it was they who revived the Torah at that time (*Yevamot* 62b).

At first glance, it is difficult to imagine how the very same individual who has come to be so identified with the principle "You shall love your neighbor as yourself" could have had vast numbers of students who failed to exemplify this concept. Furthermore, from the Talmud's point of view, these individuals suffered Divine punishment due to this deficiency, something not lost on their teacher, Rabbi Akiva.

What if as a result of this terrible loss, Rabbi Akiva first came to the realization that however much Torah his disciples were taught, if their learning does not cause them to increasingly respect and love one another, all of his and their efforts were for naught? It is entirely understandable that, initially, Rabbi Akiva may not have had his priorities straight when it came to studying Torah and conveying important ideas to his students. Rabbi Akiva first began to study when he was forty, and it is highly likely that his perspective may have been skewed. It was only after a profound national tragedy that he may have reevaluated his approach.

Might Rabbi Akiva, following this horrible loss, have embarked on a campaign to not only teach students once again, but to also, as a central part of his teachings, strive to guarantee that they should become highly sensitized to the need to show utmost deference and concern for each other? And Rabbi Akiva did not confine his realization to his own students; he emphasized this lesson at every turn before whatever audience he found himself. Consequently, being confronted with a Mishnah that describes how individuals can deliberately hurt each other by vowing against one another, Rabbi Akiva responds powerfully by advocating the centrality of Lev. 19:18, not only in the immediate context of abolishing vows, but for Judaism in general. All of this might have been based on his own first-hand tragic experience as a teacher of Torah.

Hillel's "Entire Torah" and R. Akiva's "Great Principle"

Rabbi Akiva's Marriage

Rabbinic tradition teaches that until age forty, R. Akiva was extremely unlettered in Jewish matters.[14] When Rabbi Akiva met a woman he wished to marry, his potential father-in-law, who was a wealthy man, was so opposed to the marriage that he made a vow prohibiting the couple from benefiting from his estate. Only much later, when Rabbi Akiva returned with large numbers of disciples and great reputation as well, did his father-in-law wish to revoke the vow that he had taken against his daughter and her husband.

Could this difficult experience have also formed Rabbi Akiva's attitude towards "You shall love your neighbor as yourself" in general and as a release from vows in particular?

Here is the Talmud's account:

> R. Akiva was a shepherd of Ben Kalba Savua. The latter's daughter, seeing how modest and noble [the shepherd] was,[15] said to him, "Were I to be betrothed to you, would you go away to [study at] an academy?"
>
> "Yes," he replied. She was then secretly betrothed to him and sent him away. When her father heard [what she had done] he drove her from his house and forbade her by a vow to have any benefit from his estate. He [R. Akiva] departed, and spent twelve years at the academy. When he returned home he brought with him twelve thousand disciples. [While in his home town] he heard an old man saying to her, "How long will you lead the life of a living widowhood?"
>
> "If he would listen to me," she replied, "he would spend another twelve years [studying]."

He [R. Akiva] said: "It is then with her consent that I am acting," and he departed again and spent another twelve years at the academy. When he finally returned he brought with him twenty-four thousand disciples. His wife heard [of his arrival] and went out to meet him, when her neighbors said to her, "Borrow some respectable clothes and put them on," but she replied: "A righteous man regards the life of his beast…" (Prov. 12:10).[16] On approaching him she fell upon her face and kissed his feet. His attendants were about to thrust her aside, when [R. Akiva] cried to them, "Leave her alone, mine and yours are hers."

Her father, on hearing that a great man had come to the town, said, "I shall go to him, maybe he will invalidate my vow." When he came to him [R. Akiva] asked, "Would you have made your vow if you had known that he was a great man?"

The other replied, "[Had he known] even one chapter or even one single *halakhah* [I would not have made the vow]."

He then said to him, "I am the man." The other fell upon his face and kissed his feet and also gave him half of his wealth (*Ketubot* 62b-63a).[17]

Hillel & Rabbi Akiva

It would appear that Hillel and Rabbi Akiva are describing two sides of the same coin. Rabbi Akiva cites that Lev. 19:18 stresses what one should strive to do when relating to one's fellow man, while Hillel's formulation emphasizes what one ought not to do when interacting with others.

Hillel's "Entire Torah" and R. Akiva's "Great Principle"

The words of Hillel and Rabbi Akiva apply specifically in the area of *mitzvot bein adam le-chaveiro* (commandments that regulate interpersonal behavior). This is despite the fact that many other commandments delineate how man should relate to God (*mitzvot bein adam la-Makom*). In fact, religion is typically associated with an emphasis upon worshipping God rather than only being careful in how a person treats one's fellow. Could Hillel and Rabbi Akiva be seeking to project the importance of care in interpersonal relations as a counterbalance to a common misconception?

Implications for Contemporary Jews
When looking at our own lives and how we consciously decide to practice Judaism, the emphasis that Hillel and Rabbi Akiva placed on respectful and positive interpersonal relationships is a key value. Being prepared to sacrifice one's own emotions, time, energy, and resources in favor of the proper treatment of others does not come naturally. Human beings for the most part are self-centered rather than altruistic. But if an individual defines himself as an observant Jew, he will be required to overcome his natural tendencies to focus only upon himself, or only those who are close to him, in order to extend himself to others in order to fulfill what the Torah demands.

Furthermore, when someone is concerned with demonstrating that he is learned and observant, he must realize that, according to Hillel and Rabbi Akiva, being religious carries with it the responsibility to act appropriately and even extraordinarily towards his fellow human beings. It follows that if an ostensibly religious individual falls short of this standard, all sorts of violations are incurred, and a *Chillul Hashem* (the desecration of God's Name) could very well arise.

It is also notable that if Hillel is correct when he states that the rest of the commandments are commentary, the manner in which we both study and perform *mitzvot* in general should be necessarily modified. When we study, teach, and reflect upon how to practice Torah and *mitzvot*, we should consciously strive to detect how each commandment contributes to helping us treat our fellow man in the best possible way.

Dennis Prager and Joseph Telushkin make this point when they are asked how there are observant Jews who behave immorally. They respond:

> Observance of Jewish laws between people and God does not render one more moral unless these laws are observed with the intention of becoming more moral. To expect otherwise, to expect that mechanical observance of Jewish person-to-God laws will automatically create moral individuals, is to confer upon Jewish law some magical quality which one would deem absurd if applied to any other area of life….
>
> The prophets vehemently attacked those Jews whose mechanical observance of these laws betrayed a lack of concern for the ethical principles underlying them…. The Jew who observes Jewish person-to-God laws while behaving in a reprehensible manner towards people treats these laws as exercises in ritual rather than a moral training. The result is observance which is morally, hence religiously, worthless.[18]

Hillel's "Entire Torah" and R. Akiva's "Great Principle"

Even though study is often more theoretical than practical, by repeatedly invoking the need to see how each mitzvah benefits other people or at least spares them harm, we will raise our consciousness to this issue overall, and thereby promote kindness and sensitivity.

Endnotes

1. Thinking about Hillel in this manner brings to mind one of the key distinctions that Robert Pirsig makes in his 1974 underground classic, *Zen and the Art of Motorcycle Maintenance* (pp. 9-17). A fundamental difference of opinion between the book's protagonists is whether one should understand the detailed inner workings of a motorcycle to the point that one can perform his own maintenance on the machine, or one should relate to the vehicle as an intricate working whole, leaving the particulars to a mechanic to keep the machine in good working order.

   Transferring the analogy to traditional Judaism, should one simply approach Torah and *mitzvot* as an organic whole that must be understood as one integrated totality, dependent upon the proper interactions of its ideas, values, and practices, with none playing a more central role than the others? Alternatively, is it appropriate to reflect on each part in its own right, striving to recognize how one or more may have a greater influence than the rest, thereby understanding the manner in which the elements are truly designed to achieve desired outcomes.

2. Rabbi Dr. Norman Lamm, *Faith & Doubt: Studies in Tradtional Jewish Thought*. Third Augmented Edition (Jersey City, NJ: KTAV Publishing House, 2006). Originally published in *Traditon* 9 (1967).

3. Translation from Chabad, available at the date of publication of this book at http://www.chabad.org/library/article_cdo/aid/2011/jewish/Chapter-Two.htm

4. It is generally assumed that these two Hillels are the same person.

5. John Stuart Mill, *On Liberty* (Oxford University, 1859), pp. 21-2.

6. Trans. Shlomo Pines, Volume II, University of Chicago Press, Chicago, 1974.

Hillel's "Entire Torah" and R. Akiva's "Great Principle"

7. The examples that Nachmanides offers in this comment are: "Do not go as a talebearer" (Lev. 19:16), "Do not take revenge and do not bear a grudge" (v. 16), "Do not stand idly by as the blood of your friend is spilled" (v. 16), "Do not curse the deaf" (v. 14), and, "Rise up before the elderly" (v. 32).

8. It should be noted that Nachmanides does not view this as the simple meaning of the verse, which he writes is to "[k]eep the commandments of God and His testimonies and His statutes, and by observing them intend to do the good and the right in His eyes only...." By identifying the right and the good with all the *mitzvot* of the Torah, no exclusive emphasis is placed upon either those between man and man or those between man and God.

9. *A Letter in the Scroll,* The Free Press, New York, 2000, pp. 39-40.

10. A story that the Talmud contends led to the destruction of the second Temple, contains just such a contention on the part of someone who was treated badly:

> The destruction of Jerusalem came through Kamtza and Bar Kamtza in this way. A certain man had a friend Kamtza and an enemy Bar Kamtza. He once made a party and said to his servant, "Go and bring Kamtza." The man went and brought Bar Kamtza. When the man [who hosted the party] found him there he said, "See, you tell tales about me; what are you doing here? Get out." Said the other, "Since I am here, let me stay, and I will pay you for whatever I eat and drink." He said, "I won't." "Then let me give you half the cost of the party." "No," said the other. "Then let me pay for the whole party." He still said, "No," and he took him by the hand and put him out. Said the other, "Since the Rabbis were sitting there and did not stop him, this shows

that they agreed with him. I will go and inform against them to the Government." He went and said to the Emperor, "The Jews are rebelling against you." He said, "How can I tell?" He said to him, "Send them an offering and see whether they will offer it [on the altar]." So he sent with him a fine calf. While on the way he made a blemish on its upper lip, or as some say on the white of its eye, in a place where we [Jews] count it a blemish but they do not. The Rabbis were inclined to offer it in order not to offend the Government. Said R. Zechariah b. Avkulas to them, "People will say that blemished animals are offered on the altar." They then proposed to kill Bar Kamtza so that he should not go and inform against them, but R. Zechariah b. Avkulas said to them, "Is one who makes a blemish on consecrated animals to be put to death?" R. Yochanan thereupon remarked, "Through the scrupulousness of R. Zechariah b. Abkulas our House has been destroyed, our Temple burnt, and we ourselves exiled from our land" (*Gittin* 55b-56a).

11. A similar lesson is imparted by R. Yehoshua to R. Gamliel:

When he [R. Gamliel] reached his [R. Yehoshua's] house he saw that the walls were black. He said to him: From the walls of your house it is apparent that you are a charcoal-burner. [R. Gamliel was wealthy, while R. Yehoshua was impoverished. Until he saw for himself, It had never occurred to R. Gamliel how some of his colleagues lived.] He replied: Alas for the generation of which you are the leader, seeing that you know nothing of the troubles of the scholars, their struggles to support and sustain themselves! (*Berakhot* 28a).

12. The interpretation appears as well in *Sifra Parashat Kedoshim* 2 and *Bereishit Rabbah* 24:7.

Hillel's "Entire Torah" and R. Akiva's "Great Principle"

13. Rabbi Moses Cordovero, in his classic work *Tomer Devorah* (ed. Dov HaKohen Fink, Tomer Publications, Jerusalem, 5765, p. 13) makes this point in spiritual terms. During the course of discussing the phrase *lesheeirit nachalato*,"for the remnant of His heritage" (Micah 7:18), Rabbi Cordovero writes:

> So too a person vis-à-vis his colleague. All of Israel is like blood relatives one to another, because all of their souls are a single entity. In this one is a part of that one, in that one is a part of this one....And similarly because of this reason, "All of Israel are guarantors for one another" (*Shevuot* 39a), because literally, within each one is a "limb" of the other, and when one sins, he harms not only himself but also the portion of his colleague which is within him. Consequently, because of that portion, his colleague is a guarantor for him and they are as if blood relatives....

14. Two teachings about Rabbi Akiva's early life are as follows:

> What were the beginnings of R. Akiva? They said he was forty years old and hadn't learned anything. Once, he was standing at the mouth of a well. He said: "Who engraved this stone?" They said to him: "The water that continually falls upon it every day"... Immediately R. Akiva drew a logical conclusion regarding himself—Just as something soft [water] can chisel that which is hard [stone], the words of Torah that are as strong as steel all the more so will be able to make an impression upon my heart which is comprised of flesh and blood. Immediately he went to study Torah... (*Avot de-Rabbi Natan*, chapter 6).

Another teaching:

> It was taught, R. Akiva said: "When I was uneducated, I said: 'I would that I had a scholar [before me], and I would maul him

like an ass.'" Said his disciples to him: "Rabbi, say like a dog!" "The former bites and breaks the bones, while the latter bites but does not break the bones," he answered them (*Pesachim* 49b).

15. It would appear that there is an inconsistency between Rachel's very positive evaluation of R. Akiva's character, and the ferocious description R. Akiva gave of himself in *Pesachim* 49b. She obviously recognized the potential of which Rabbi Akiva himself may have been unaware.

16. The verse is quoted in both *Ketubot* and *Nedarim* and attributed to R. Akiva's wife describing herself. For Rachel to apply to herself the term *behemah* (beast/domesticated animal) appears to be extremely subservient. While she may have seen herself as the ultimate enabler—according to the Talmud, it was due to her specific urging that Rabbi Akiva left her for twenty-four years of concentrated Torah study—shouldn't that have been a badge of honor rather than cause for personal disparagement? Perhaps the text has to be interpreted as a form of *kal vachomer* (reasoning from a minor case to a major one) that if a *tzaddik* will be by definition extremely concerned about his animals, it goes without saying that he will be concerned for my welfare and dignity. And her expectation was borne out.

17. A more concise version of this story appears in *Nedarim* 50a. Of particular note is that according to this second version, it is specifically the 24,000 disciples who try to prevent Rachel from rejoining her husband, evidencing once again a lacking in terms of the appreciation of "And you shall love your neighbor as yourself."

18. "How Do You Account for Religious Jews Who are Unethical?" in Telushkin and Prager, *Nine Questions that People Ask About Judaism*, Touchstone, New York, 1975, pp. 68-69.

Chapter 2

Ben Azzai's Central Principle

תלמוד ירושלמי (וילנא) מסכת נדרים פרק ט הלכה ד
[ויקרא יט יח] "ואהבת לרעך כמוך" . רבי עקיבה אומר זהו כלל גדול
בתורה. בן עזאי אומר [בראשית ה א] "זה ספר תולדות אדם..." —
זה כלל גדול מזה.

Jerusalem Talmud *Nedarim* 9:4
"You shall love your neighbor as yourself" (Lev. 19:18). R. Akiva says, "This is the central principle [*kelal gadol*] of the Torah." Ben Azzai says: "This is the book of the generations of man/Adam[1] [in the day that God Created man, in the likeness of God made He him]"[2] (Gen. 5:1)—this is an even greater principle.

בראשית רבה (וילנא) פרשת בראשית פרשה כד סימן ז
שלא תאמר הואיל ונתבזיתי יתבזה חבירי עמי הואיל ונתקללתי
יתקלל חבירי עמי.

Genesis Rabbah 24:7
That you should not say, "Since I disparage myself, let my colleague be disparaged with me," or, "Since I cursed myself, let my colleague be cursed with me."

The Life of Ben Azzai

Ben Azzai's full name was Rabbi Shimon ben Azzai. Rabbi Akiva was probably older than Ben Azzai, but the two knew each other and directly interacted with one another. Rabbi Akiva was not Ben Azzai's teacher, but the latter certainly drew great wisdom from him. In one place, Ben Azzai regrets that he did not stand in closer relation as a pupil to Rabbi Akiva (*Nedarim* 74b). In his halakhic opinions and biblical exegesis, Ben Azzai frequently follows Rabbi Akiva, although in this famous case Ben Azzai breaks from his elder's tradition.

Ben Azzai's Alternative Central Principle

The central rule advocated by Rabbi Akiva, "And you shall love your neighbor as yourself" (Lev. 19:18) is widely known, and has even been set to music.[3] However, Ben Azzai's position, "This is the book of the generations of man/Adam," which presents itself as a counterproposal to what Rabbi Akiva says, appears to be far more prosaic. There are three places where this pair of opinions, attributed to Rabbi Akiva and Ben Azzai, is quoted.[4]

Studying Both Views

Hillel's explanation of what constitutes *kol ha-Torah kullah* (the entire Torah) does not have a conflicting view in that story. The absence of a contrasting point of view limits the depth of understanding that can be achieved. The claim of Rabbi Akiva, however, is accompanied by dissonance and debate. While Rabbi Akiva's opinion shares some features with Hillel's central principle, Ben Azzai's dissenting opinion allows for all the positions to be understood with greater clarity.

Ben Azzai's Central Principle

The Benefits of Ben Azzai's Approach

At first glance, it appears that the dispute between Rabbi Akiva and Ben Azzai regarding the essence of the Torah and Judaism concerns which group of commandments is of greatest importance. Rabbi Akiva appears to advocate for the centrality of rules governing interpersonal relationships (Lev. 19:18), while Ben Azzai emphasizes attitudes and actions associated with the relationship between man and God (Gen. 5:1), in the realization that all men are creatures of God, the Creator, and are formed in His image.

This dichotomy can be observed in a number of rabbinic sources. For example:

> R. Shimon the Just was one of the remaining members of the Men of the Great Assembly. He used to say: On three things the world stands: on Torah, service [between man and God] and on acts of kindness [interpersonal laws] (*Avot* 1:2).[5]

> Rav Yehudah said: One who wishes to be pious must fulfill the laws of *Nezikin* [torts, hence interpersonal laws]. But Rava said: The matters of *Avot* [which can be categorized as personal refinement, *bein adam le-atzmo*]. Still others said: matters of *Berakhot* [blessings, i.e., between man and God] (*Bava Kamma* 30a).

> Said Rava, R. Idi explained it to me: "Say of the righteous, when he is good, that they shall eat the fruit of their doings" (Isa. 3:10). Is there then a righteous man who is good, and a righteous man who is not good? But he who is

good to Heaven and good to man), he is a righteous man who is good. Good to Heaven but not good to man, that is a righteous man who is not good.

Similarly you read: "Woe unto the wicked [who is] evil; for the reward of his hands shall be given unto him" (v. 11). Is there then a wicked man that is evil and one that is not evil? But he that is evil to Heaven and evil to man, he is a wicked man that is evil. He who is evil to Heaven but not evil to man, he is a wicked man that is not evil (*Kiddushin* 40a).

In Chapter 1 we noted that Hillel's as well as Rabbi Akiva's emphasis upon interpersonal relationships did not appear to be spiritual, let alone Jewish. The same cannot be said for Ben Azzai, with his focus upon God and, implicitly, the specifically Jewish conception of God. Furthermore, it must be noted that Ben Azzai is given the last word in the text, without a response from Rabbi Akiva or anyone else attempting to defend Lev. 19:18.

In *Genesis Rabbah* only Ben Azzai, and not R. Akiva, offers a rationale to further advance his viewpoint. It seems that Ben Azzai's opinion prevails even though it is not as well-known.

Ben Azzai's Personality

The Talmud presents Ben Azzai as an individual who was completely and entirely devoted to God (*kullo Lashem*). He possessed a single-minded commitment to Torah study to the point that he did not even marry. The following exchange is recorded:

> It was taught: R. Eliezer stated: He who does not engage in propagation of the race is as though he sheds blood; for it is

said, "Whoever sheds man's blood, by man shall his blood be shed" (Gen. 9:6), and this is immediately followed by the verse, "And you shall be fruitful and multiply" (v. 7). R. Yaakov said: As though he has diminished the Divine image; since it is said, "For in the image of God made He man" (v. 6), and this is immediately followed by, "And you shall be fruitful...."

Ben Azzai said: As though he sheds blood *and* diminishes the Divine image; since it is said, "And you, be ye fruitful and multiply" [following both of these clauses in the preceding verse].

They said to Ben Azzai: Some preach well and act well, others act well but do not preach well; you, however, preach well but do not act well [Ben Azzai didn't marry]. Ben Azzai replied: But what shall I do, seeing that my soul is in love with the Torah? The world can be carried on by others (*Yevamot* 63b).

From this passage, it seems that Ben Azzai never even wished to marry. Another passage might demonstrate that Ben Azzai was ambivalent about this matter or that he had a change of heart at a certain point. Apparently he was prepared to marry the daughter of his teacher and colleague Rabbi Akiva, but once she agreed that he should first spend significant time studying Torah, as had her mother before her, Ben Azzai ultimately decided not to marry:[6]

> The daughter of Rabbi Akiva acted in a similar way towards Ben Azzai. This is indeed an illustration of the proverb: "Ewe follows ewe; a daughter's acts are like those of her mother" (*Ketubot* 63a).

The Great Principle of the Torah

The passage that probably most powerfully reflects Ben Azzai's attraction to otherworldliness and his primary devotion to spiritual matters is the mystical image of the four who entered Pardes, the spiritual orchard:

> Our Rabbis taught: Four men entered Pardes: Ben Azzai, Ben Zoma, Acher,[7] and R. Akiva. R. Akiva said to them: When you arrive at the stones of pure marble, say not, "Water, water!" For it is said, "He that speaks falsehood shall not be established before My Eyes" (Psalm 101:7). Ben Azzai cast a look and died. Of him Scripture says: "Precious in the sight of the Lord is the death of His saints" (Psalm 116:15). Ben Zoma looked and became demented. Of him Scripture says: "Have you found honey? Eat so much as is sufficient for you, lest you be filled therewith, and vomit it" (Prov. 25:16). Acher mutilated the shoots [lost his faith]. R. Akiva departed unhurt (*Chagigah* 14b).

A possible interpretation would maintain that Rabbi Akiva was grounded in this world to such an extent that his relationships with others prevented him from totally losing himself in God and spirituality, hence his advocacy for "And you shall love your neighbor as yourself" (Lev. 19:18). Ben Azzai, on the other hand, was drawn to that which was transcendent, to the point that when he was exposed to what lay beyond, he lost himself and no longer desired to participate in this world.[8] For him, recognizing that one is created in the image of God becomes paramount, and at least for Ben Azzai himself, a focus upon Godliness could even lead one to reject this world's everyday existence.

Three Interpretations of Ben Azzai's Statement

However otherworldly Ben Azzai's outlook may seem to be, it would appear that commentaries are not in agreement concerning whether a dichotomy actually exists between him and Rabbi Akiva regarding the relative importance of commandments between man and God, as opposed to interpersonal commandments. We will consider three interpretations: those of the *Korban ha-Edah*, the *Pnei Moshe*, and Rabbi Samson Raphael Hirsch.

The *Korban ha-Edah*'s Two Interpretations

The *Korban ha-Edah* (Rabbi David ben Rabbi Naphtali Hirsch Frankel, 1707-1762) is one of the primary commentaries on the Jerusalem Talmud. He offers two interpretations of Ben Azzai's statement (s.v., *zeh sefer toldot Adam*).

First, "This is the book of the generations of Adam"—all human beings come from a single person, Adam the first man.

Second, the *Korban ha-Edah* records that some people interpret Ben Azzai as focusing on the end of the verse, "in the likeness [*demut*] of God made He him" (Gen. 5:1). For this reason it is proper to be careful regarding how a person interacts with another.

The strength of the first interpretation is that those are the words that Ben Azzai actually quoted, "This is the book of the generations of Adam." The second interpretation highlights the use of the word *demut*, "likeness," which Rashi understands as the intellectual capacity of man.

The *Korban ha-Edah*'s First Interpretation: Common Ancestry

In his first explanation of Ben Azzai, the *Korban ha-Edah* offers an objective, universalistic perspective—all of humanity is descended from a single individual, Adam the first man (*Adam ha-Rishon*). By definition we are all related and ought to sense that we owe one another the sort of deference and respect that applies to one's family members.[9] In fact, Ben Azzai is more universal than Rabbi Akiva, since it was noted in Chapter 1 that Rabbi Akiva's view applies only to Jews, while Ben Azzai's view encompasses all of humanity.

Ben Azzai's reasoning emphasizes a biological relationship that defines all human beings as sharing a common origin. This view is reminiscent of one of the concepts by which witnesses in a capital case are adjured prior to their giving testimony in order to attempt to impress upon them how serious it is to accuse someone of a crime punishable by death, as described in a Mishnah:

> Therefore was man created from a single individual to teach you… peace among people, that one individual should not say to another, "My father was greater than yours" (*Sanhedrin* 4:5).

The *Korban ha-Edah*'s Second Interpretation: Shared Spirituality

In his alternate explanation, the *Korban ha-Edah* turns to the concluding portion of the verse for what he proposes is Ben Azzai's lesson, and states that since all human beings are created in the image of God, they are all deserving of fair treatment and respect. This view emphasizes the spiritual relationship that we all share with one another. It suggests that human beings must treat each other as if each person is a holy entity, i.e., the spiritual quality with which each person is endowed.

Ironically, it is Rabbi Akiva himself, Ben Azzai's disputant, who articulates this view concisely in a Mishnah:

He [R. Akiva] also used to say: Beloved is man in that he was created in the image of God. It is a mark of superabundant love that it was made known to him that he had been created in the image of God, as it is said, "for in the image of God made He man" (Gen. 9:6).

Beloved are Israel in that they were called children of the All-Present. It was a mark of superabundant love that it was made known to them that they were called children of the All-Present, as it is said, "You are children of the Lord your God" (*Avot* 3:14, quoting Deut. 14:1).

Comparing the *Korban ha-Edah*'s Two Views

Upon comparing the two explanations for Ben Azzai's view proposed by *Korban ha-Edah*, one could contend that the second explanation is more far-reaching and impactful than the first. Biological unity is diluted over time, as we have to go back in history in order to identify the common ancestor from whom humanity began. Nevertheless, each person always remains a physical entity unto himself, even if he happens to be related to others by virtue of his genetic makeup. Rabbi Joseph B. Soloveitchik has emphasized that though all mankind shares a common ancestor, the differences are terribly great, to the point that communication is often difficult:

> The word is a paradoxical instrument of communication and contains an inner contradiction. On the one hand, the word is the medium of expressing agreement and concurrence, of reaching mutual understanding, organizing cooperative effort, and uniting action. On the other hand, the word is also the means of manifesting distinctness, emphasizing incongruity, and underlining

separateness. The word brings out not only what is common in two existences but the singularity and uniqueness of each existence as well.[10]

Thus, however much one may argue that each human being is similar, there are numerous profound differences as well.

On the other hand, when asserting that it is the likeness of God that is humanity's common denominator, this is a spiritual, non-material quality that one believes should inform people's sensibilities and natures at all times for all individuals. An awareness of another's *tzelem Elokim* (image of God) does not require historical sensitivity; it is a religious existential reality of human beings' essential natures.

It would appear from the *Korban ha-Edah*'s approach that Ben Azzai is merely adding an additional dimension to Rabbi Akiva's view, rather than fundamentally disagreeing with it. Though Ben Azzai prefers Gen. 5:1 to make the point, but in terms of emphasis, both R. Akiva and Ben Azzai end up being in agreement.

The *Pnei Moshe*'s Interpretation:
Human Interaction as Worship

The other standard commentary on the Jerusalem Talmud is the *Pnei Moshe* (Rabbi Moshe ben Rabbi Shimon Margalit, 1710-1780). The *Pnei Moshe* believes that Ben Azzai is emphasizing the second half of Gen. 5:1, and advances conclusions that reflect a markedly different perspective than the *Korban ha-Edah*:

> Because of its end was this verse cited [by Ben Azzai], where it is written, "in the likeness of God made He him." And when a person reflects on this, he will be very

careful regarding the honor of another. And as it is said in *Genesis Rabbah*, "And if you do so [disparage another human being], realize Whom you are disparaging—'in the likeness of God made He him'" (*Genesis Rabbah* 24:7).[11]

[This phrase] includes two issues [that make it central]: [First] that when a person is careful regarding the honor of another person, he is also protecting the honor of his Creator, since he is in the likeness of God. [Second] and all the more so he will be careful about trespassing against God, as well as be diligent in the performance of commandments as yet another means to give honor to the Blessed One (*Pnei Moshe*, s.v. *zeh sefer toldot ha-Adam zeh kelal gadol mi-zeh*).

The *Pnei Moshe*, instead of stressing the social, universalistic and interpersonal implications of "image of God" (*demut Elokim*), focuses on it as a concept between man and God (*bein adam la-Makom*). He implies that for Ben Azzai, the true central principle of Judaism is respecting and worshipping God. Such an interpretation would have Ben Azzai squarely contradicting both Rabbi Akiva and Hillel, who ranked interpersonal relationships as the highest priority.

Such a religious attitude can best be achieved by viewing all human beings as manifestations of some aspect of the Divine. Properly interacting with them therefore offers continual opportunities to show respect for God indirectly, which in turn should lead to a heightened awareness of the need to demonstrate deference and respect for God directly.

Furthermore, according to the *Pnei Moshe*'s perspective, the appropriate treatment of those with whom one comes into contact, becomes a system of reminders of God's Presence and a means of intensifying a person's awareness of God. Paradoxically, care in interpersonal relationships achieves a goal similar to the performance of specific ritual commandments. If in ritual commandments one is often dealing with a "mitzvah object" (*cheftza shel mitzvah*, like *tefillin*, *shofar*, *lulav*, or Hanukkah candles), when dealing with other human beings, each person becomes a "mitzvah object" as well. Normal social activity presents one with many more occasions to be reminded of God and the obligations that we have towards Him, than do carefully fulfilling ritual observances, which are rarer. There are restricted times for *tefillin* and *shofar*, but there is no limit to the amount that people can interact, and each encounter is an opportunity to be reminded of the presence of God.

Nachmanides appears to loosely support the *Pnei Moshe*'s approach, when he remarks passionately and movingly about why so many commandments appear to be associated with the Exodus from Egypt, as well as about what the overarching purpose of the totality of commandments may be:

> [The Sages] said, "Be as careful to fulfill a minor commandment as a major one…" (*Avot* 2:1). Because they are all very dear and beloved, because at every moment, an individual affirms through their performance his belief in his God, and the intention of all commandments is that we believe in our God and affirm to Him that He is our Creator, that this was the intention of the Creation, for we have no other explanation for the original Creation, and the exalted God desires nothing from the lower ones [i.e., mankind] other than that man know and affirm his God

and his Creator (Nachmanides on Exod. 13:16, s.v., *u-le-totafot bein einekha*).

According to the *Pnei Moshe*'s understanding of Ben Azzai, interpersonal and ritual commandments in the end accomplish the same end that Nachmanides points out—to acknowledge and worship God.

Rabbi Samson Raphael Hirsch's Interpretation: Man's Essential Nature

Rabbi Samson Raphael Hirsch (1808-1888) presents a third understanding of Ben Azzai's proposal. In his commentary on Gen. 5:1, Rabbi Hirsch understands the opening phrase of the verse as, "This is the book of the generations of man." That is, *adam* refers to all mankind, not specifically the first man. Rabbi Hirsch says this phrase should be understood as: "This is the record of all of the doings of man (for good and for bad) once he was created in the likeness of God."

Man, by definition, due to his freedom of choice,[12] has the potential to be either superior to the angels,[13] or more corrupt than the greatest perpetrator of evil among other creatures, or anything in between. Therefore human behaviors should be viewed as manifestations of different points along the moral and spiritual spectrum inherent within man's nature from the moment of his creation. The verse makes us view mankind as a unified whole, considering all behaviors as true manifestations of man's essential potential and nature.

Consequently Rabbi Hirsch presents Ben Azzai as neither emphasizing man's biological or spiritual unity, nor his fundamental need to serve God indirectly and directly. He believes that Ben Azzai demands that we should not allow our negative moral judgment of someone's behavior to lead us to deny his basic humanity. Furthermore, we ought to recognize our own innate capacities to do admirable, heroic things, similar to those carried out by exemplary individuals. As a consequence, as we read the "case studies" of biblical personalities contained in the Torah, we should not assume that the level of righteous individuals is unattainable, nor believe that only a very small number of people can achieve great spiritual and moral accomplishments. Rather we should perceive that each of us has such capabilities if we would only undertake to realize them. Similarly, evil-doers are not a species unto themselves, but act in ways in which we are all potentially capable, should we choose to forsake proper self-discipline and moral and spiritual reflection and personal striving.

Perhaps God Himself summarizes best the range of human capabilities when He confronts Cain following the Divine rejection of his sacrifice in favor of that of his younger brother Abel: "If you do well, shall you not be lifted up? And if you do not do well, sin crouches at the door; and unto you is its desire, but you may rule over it" (Gen. 4:7). This verse gives three distinct ideas: someone who behaves well will be raised up, someone who acts poorly will always be confronted with sin, but the choice is for man to take ownership of his life.

Rabbi Hirsch contends that even though Cain murdered his brother, this horrific act was not inevitable and could have been obviated by an act of will-power and personal commitment. Consequently, if we are not careful, we too, as a result of some extreme fit of anger or unbridled passion, are capable of acting like Cain.

Ben Azzai's Central Principle

An example of the converse of Cain's behavior, where individuals demonstrate the highest level of idealism and moral conviction, is embodied in the behavior of the midwives assigned to assist Jewish women giving birth in Egypt:

> And the king of Egypt spoke to the Hebrew midwives, of whom the name of the one was Shifra, and the name of the other Puah; and he said: "When you serve as a midwife for the Hebrew women, you shall look upon the birth stool: if it be a son, then you shall kill him; but if it be a daughter, then she shall live." But the midwives feared God, and did not as the king of Egypt commanded them, but saved the male-children alive. And the king of Egypt called for the midwives, and said unto them: "Why have you done this thing, and saved the male-children alive?" And the midwives said unto Pharaoh: "Because the Hebrew women are not as the Egyptian women; for they are lively, and are delivered before the midwife come to them." And God dealt well with the midwives; and the people multiplied, and waxed very mighty. And it came to pass, because the midwives feared God, that He made them houses (Exod. 1:15-21).

While many might think that they would lack the courage displayed by these women in standing up to the commands of the Egyptian monarch, Rabbi Hirsch's view of Ben Azzai's "central principle" would maintain that we all have the capacity to act heroically in the manner of the midwives; the only question is whether or not we wish to. Consequently, the Torah constitutes an inventory of human capabilities that we should take to heart in order to know ourselves better and thereby strive for goodness and holiness.

The Great Principle of the Torah

Rabbi Akiva and Ben Azzai Compared

Whenever there is a dispute in the Talmud, it is fair to assume that each individual is aware of the perspective advocated by his disputant. Each side therefore feels that his proposal addresses and improves upon some issue overlooked or deemphasized by his counterpart. Applying such a line of reasoning to the dispute between Rabbi Akiva and Ben Azzai, what might be the strengths and weaknesses of each view?

Analyzing Rabbi Akiva's Interpretation

Rabbi Akiva, in drawing attention to the phrase, "And you shall love your neighbor as yourself" has captured the popular imagination. It is a statement that addresses our emotions, and it is terse and to the point; its takeaway message is immediately comprehensible. Since its focus is upon our dealings with other human beings, it discusses an experience that is accessible, ubiquitous, and not necessarily intuitive.

Human beings, like other sentient creatures, are instinctively motivated to advance self-preservation. Worrying about one's own comfort and survival usually puts one at odds with others whose needs are competing with our own. To overcome these natural tendencies requires idealism and self-sacrifice, qualities that do not come naturally to most people. A statement like "You shall love your neighbor as yourself" highlights the need for going beyond what comes naturally.[14]

Rabbi Akiva might dismiss Ben Azzai's proposal as too cerebral and intellectual. Whereas *Parashat Kedoshim* (Lev. 19:1-20:27) in general, and Lev. 19:18 in particular, literally leap out at the reader and capture his attention and imagination, most people would have never considered Gen. 5:1 as a key verse in the Torah, let alone the most fundamental of Torah concepts. Furthermore, Lev. 19:18 is in the form of a commandment, while Gen. 5:1 is part of a descriptive, historical narrative.

Analyzing Ben Azzai's Interpretation

The Midrash explains Ben Azzai as a level higher than Rabbi Akiva: "That you should not say, 'Since I disparage myself, let my colleague be disparaged with me'; 'Since I cursed myself, let my colleague be cursed with me'" (*Genesis Rabbah* 24:7). Ben Azzai feels that Lev. 19:18 is overly dependent upon the state of mind and the self-esteem of the individual to whom the commandment is directed. The word *kamokha*, "as yourself," leaves open the possibility that if someone does not mind being disparaged or abused, he might think that he has license, in turn, to act in this manner towards others.[15]

According to the *Korban ha-Edah*, Ben Azzai may disagree on two different levels with Rabbi Akiva's rule. Whether one emphasizes the first or the second portion of Gen. 5:1, a much greater universe of people are being included than what is implied by Lev. 19:18. Whereas the latter is limited to one's neighbor (i.e., a Jew), Ben Azzai is interested in respect being given to all of humanity, either because of biological or spiritual considerations.

The *Pnei Moshe* might frame the disagreement between Rabbi Akiva and Ben Azzai as a question of whether interpersonal commandments or ritual (between man and God) commandments are the most basic elements within Judaism and the Torah. Since at the end of the day all commandments are incumbent upon the observant individual, the debate could be about the best way to tell if an individual, or for that matter, oneself, is properly growing spiritually. How is the religious individual to be evaluated—by how he ultimately relates to God or how he interacts with his fellow human beings? Put another way, what is the best way to access Judaism—developing a heightened God-sensibility that will result in treating everyone created in God's image with great respect, or being sensitive to one's fellow man, which in turn will lead to greater sensitivity about God.

Rabbi Hirsch assumes that in order to be a central principle, what should be dealt with is some all-encompassing principle about human behavior that can lead to understanding humanity as a whole, rather than a specific call to act in a certain manner, whether towards God or one's fellow man. He maintains that to understand how others act is more important than to focus upon the manner in which one acts oneself.

Implications for Contemporary Jews
When confronted by this disagreement between Rabbi Akiva (and Hillel) on the one hand, and Ben Azzai on the other, it is possible to affirm and recommend several seemingly different points of view simultaneously. The phrase, *eilu ve-eilu divrei Elokim chaim*, "these and these are the words of the living God," can aptly be applied in this particular instance, as we seek to formulate practical, contemporary implications arising from these positions and interpretations. We can acknowledge that there is inherent truth in both opinions without being forced to advance one opinion over the other.

Hillel and Rabbi Akiva powerfully contend that positive interactions with our fellow man are a paramount criterion for determining if an observant Jew was acting properly. Ben Azzai (at least according to the *Korban ha-Edah*) augments—rather than contradicts—Rabbi Akiva by turning our attention to why

Ben Azzai's Central Principle

		Rabbi Akiva		Ben Azzai	
		Strengths	Weaknesses	Strengths	Weaknesses
	Korban ha-Edah	Emotional (appeals to a person's emotions)	Subjective (assumes person has self-respect)	Cognitive: (a) biological connection or (b) spiritual connection	Too abstract
	Pnei Moshe	Respect everyone	Respect only as much as one respect's oneself	Good interpersonal behavior honors God indirectly	No inherent value in interpersonal laws
	Rabbi Samson Raphael Hirsch	Emphasizes the good in man, not the bad when one seeks only to do good to one's fellow	Less comprehensive than Ben Azzai's opinion	Acknowledges man's capacity for both good and evil	A great rule is a directive for behavior, rather than a description of human nature

proper interpersonal treatment is important. The *Korban ha-Edah* suggests that to ensure that we treat all people with the respect advocated by Hillel and Rabbi Akiva, we must look upon fellow human beings as either literally family or inherently holy.

With the gradual societal acceptance of multiculturalism beginning in the 1960's, general society has been increasingly viewed as an aggregate of various ethnic, cultural, and religious groups that often don't share the same language or basic values with one another. To expect individuals to relate to their fellow citizens, even their co-religionists—when considering denominational, economic, and political divisions—as family members and equivalent embodiments of holiness, constitutes a huge challenge to the natural and common sensibilities of even the most learned and spiritual individuals.

In light of this, should we posit that while Hillel, Rabbi Akiva, and the *Korban ha-Edah*'s understanding of Ben Azzai may be eminently correct as ideals, realizing such a standard is well beyond the reach of the average traditional Jew today? Alternatively, should the observant individual as well as the Jewish community at large embark upon a massive reeducation program to bring themselves in line with this central principle? If we are to do so, should Ben Azzai's perspective be given greater public attention? In addition, the overall question of how we view our fellow man becomes a crucial component in our religious and educational initiatives.

According to the *Pnei Moshe*, Ben Azzai takes issue with Hillel and Rabbi Akiva. While the latter claim that excellence in interpersonal commandments is the most important goal of Judaism, the *Pnei Moshe* argues that Ben Azzai differs radically. The point of all commandments, even those that are ostensibly interpersonal, is to sensitize ourselves to God.

Ben Azzai's Central Principle

The disagreement could be one of emphasis. Even though all commandments are meant to be observed, the point of reference can differ. We can excel in interpersonal dealings as a function of our belief in God, or we can use our interpersonal dealings to give honor to God. This is the debate between the *Korban ha-Edah* and the *Pnei Moshe* in understanding Ben Azzai. If we assume that there is sufficient time and energy to try to master both areas of religious life, then the dispute is more pyrrhic than substantive. But in terms of the "economy of the curriculum,"[16] as well as the limited time that ordinary individuals have to study Torah, the disagreement has very practical implications. What should I devote myself to the most: theology, ritual law, understanding how God interacts with man in history, or interpersonal relationships, the laws of gossip and slander, the laws of charity, the parameters of taking an active part in the affairs of the community? What is of tantamount importance? Which perspective is most likely to positively affect the other?

Rabbi Hirsch's take on Ben Azzai constitutes a synthesis between the *Korban ha-Edah* and *Pnei Moshe*. When I consider how all of human activity reflects the range of possibility that human capacity encompasses, to what extent should I be judgmental regarding shortcomings in another's behavior, both in interpersonal and ritual laws? How can I best inspire myself and others by becoming aware of exemplary cases of people fulfilling the highest levels of these two different types of commandments? Regularly reading biographies[17] of spiritual luminaries may be one practical way of thinking about what human beings are actually capable of. But acquainting oneself with the remarkable acts of *chesed* on the part of relatively ordinary individuals, as is exemplified in Rabbi Jonathan Sacks' book *To Heal a Fractured*

World: The Ethics of Responsibility,[18] would also go a long way toward furthering this ideal.

An additional difference between the commentators is what constitutes the source of one's conclusions regarding the central rule of the Torah—do I acquire knowledge regarding what I should and should not be doing from abstract formulations and hortatory teachings, or is my learning derived from studying the living as well as recorded examples of how others live their lives, for better or worse?

Ben Azzai's Central Principle

Endnotes

1. Among the commentators, there are those who understand the word *adam* as connoting the generic human being, while others specifically refer to the first man, Adam.

2. In this selection from the Talmud, as is often the case, only the beginning of a verse is cited, and the reader is expected to fill in the missing words. Certainly in this instance, it is possible that Ben Azzai's proposed "greater principle" is specifically based upon the end of the verse, which the Talmud assumes that the reader will complete from memory. On the other hand, the *Korban ha-Edah* offers two explanations for Ben Azzai (which are shown later in this chapter), the first of which focuses upon only the portion of the verse that appears in the Talmud, rather than the unstated second portion.

3. "*Ve-ahavta le-reiakha kamokha—zeh kelal gadol ba-Torah*" has been put to music and rendered into popular songs any number of times. The same cannot be said for "*Zeh sefer toldot Adam.*"

4. The two views are each found in Yerushalmi *Nedarim* 9:4; *Sifra Kedoshim* 2; and *Genesis Rabbah* 24:7. However they are not presented in the same order.

> "You shall love your neighbor as yourself" (Lev. 19:18). R. Akiva says, "This is the central principle [*kelal gadol*] of the Torah." Ben Azzai says: "This is the book of the generations of man/Adam [in the day that God created man, in the likeness of God made He him]" (Gen. 5:1)—this is an even greater principle (Yerushalmi *Nedarim* 9:4).

In *Genesis Rabbah* 24:7, which is a direct comment on Gen. 5:1, Ben Azzai is cited first, R. Akiva second, with the subsequent discussion focusing exclusively on Ben Azzai without any elaboration of R. Akiva:

The Great Principle of the Torah

> Ben Azzai says, "This is the book of the generations of man..."—this is the great principle [*kelal gadol*] in the Torah. R. Akiva says, "...And you shall love your neighbor as yourself..."—this is the great [*kelal gadol*; the Midrash does not say Rabbi Akiva's opinion is greater] principle in the Torah. That you should not say, "Since I will allow myself to be disparaged, let my friend be disparaged with me"; "Since I will allow myself to be cursed, let my friend be cursed with me." Said R. Tanchuma: If you do this, know Whom you are disparaging, "... In the likeness of God made He him."

The comment "That you should not say..." cannot be an explication of Rabbi Akiva's view, since according to him, you should only love your neighbor as much as yourself, which suggests that if you do not love yourself, you may be permitted to act poorly towards your neighbor. Unquestionably, R. Tanchuma's addition further strengthens Ben Azzai's position. It should not be surprising that in a source that focuses on Gen. 5:1, Ben Azzai's view is most fully explicated. In the two other sources, the Yerushalmi and the *Sifra*, these views are not as well developed.

5. This Mishnah has three categories, not two. Divine service (*avodah*) is between man and God, while "acts of kindness" means interpersonal commandments. According to some commentaries, the use of "Torah" here refers to a third area which Judaism attempts to influence positively, i.e., *bein adam le-atzmo* (between man and himself). It is possible that Torah study is intended for this type of self-development and personal growth. On the other hand, Torah study can be seen to help an individual understand what his responsibilities are for both interpersonal and ritual laws.

6. Tosafot raises the seeming contradiction, since one source has Ben Azzai discussing the nature of intimacy, while another source says he never married:

Ben Azzai's Central Principle

And if you ask, in the first chapter of *Sotah* (4b) it states that Ben Azzai never married, but they [those discussing the nature of sexual intimacy] included Ben Azzai, who was unmarried. If you wish I can say that he married and separated [from his wife, which means *Yevamot* criticizes him only for not having children]; or he had heard it [about the nature of intimacy] from his master [rather than experiencing it first-hand]; or "That the secret of the Lord is with them that fear him" (Psalm 25:15) [Ben Azzai came to this knowledge via Divine Revelation] (Tosafot, *Ketubot* 63a, s.v. *barteih de-R. Akiva*).

Tosafot offers three views. First is that he did marry but didn't have children. Second, he never married but learned about intimacy from his teacher. Third, the nature of intimacy was revealed through prophecy.

According to the first view there is no contradiction; he discussed intimacy because he had been married. But it is also possible that even though it is stated in *Ketubot* that he married, he only did *eirusin* (halakhic engagement) not *nesuin* (halakhic marriage), so he never consummated.

7. Elisha ben Avuya. Due to his losing his faith, he was called Acher ("someone else") because he no longer resembled the individual who previously had been a great scholar and member of the *Sanhedrin*.

8. Thinking about Ben Azzai and R. Akiva in this manner has always reminded me of the following story associated with the Baal Shem Tov:

People would come to him every day, sharing with him their complaints, or asking him to help them with their needs in life. He would comfort them all, but in the evening his restless soul would free itself in pursuit of the otherworldly, and would enter heaven. In heaven there is no time, only timelessness. But each morning his soul returned to his own bed. This happened every night until finally his soul was given a choice—either push further into heaven and withdraw from the world, or turn back and remain involved in physical existence. The soul began to speak, "I detach myself from—"

A woman bends over a bed and says, "Israel," using the given name of the Baal Shem Tov, and the soul turned back. That was the last time the master journeyed to heaven.

See Martin Buber's *The Legend of the Baal Shem*, "The Heavenly Journey" trans. Maurice Friedman (New York: Schocken, 1955), pp. 79-81.

9. It is troubling how often, particularly in the book of Genesis, family members treat each other terribly:

- Cain commits fratricide (Gen. 4:8);
- Ham exploits his father's drunken nakedness (9:22;
- Ishmael mocks his younger brother (21:9);
- Abraham banishes Hagar and Ishmael (21:14);
- Jacob attempts to gain the upper hand over his brother (25:29-34; 27:18-30);
- Jacob shows favoritism with his wives and children (29:31; 33:2; 37:3-4);
- Laban cheats his nephew (29:23; 31:1-2; 31:41);
- The brothers treat Joseph with hostility (37:8, 11, 20 ff).

It should not be surprising, especially based on the stories of Genesis, that the Torah highlights how caring we are required to be towards members of our family. These include:

- Parents
  - Respecting them (Exod. 20:12; Deut. 5:16);
  - Fearing them (Lev. 19:3);
  - Not cursing them (Exod. 21:17, Lev. 20:9, Deut. 27:16);
  - Not striking them (Exod. 21:15).
- Immediate family members (parents, siblings, children) on whose behalves one must become ritually impure during the course of seeing to their burial (Lev. 21:2-3).

- Children
  - Teaching them Torah (Deut. 6:7, which may include all students);
  - Imparting to them lessons of the Exodus (Exod. 10:2; 13:8, 14; Deut. 6:20);
  - The stubborn and rebellious child (i.e., proper educational methods, Deut. 21:18-21)

10. R. Joseph Soloveitchik, "Confrontation" (*Tradition*, Spring-Summer 1964).

11. A powerful anecdote that literally illustrates this perspective appears in the Talmud:

> Our Rabbis have taught: A man should always be gentle as the reed and never unyielding as the cedar.
>
> Once R. Eleazar son of R. Shimon was coming from Migdal Gedor, from the house of his teacher, and he was riding leisurely on his donkey by the riverside and was feeling happy and elated because he had studied much Torah. There chanced to meet him an exceedingly ugly man who greeted him, "Peace be upon you, sir." He, however, did not return his salutation but instead said to him, "*Raika* (lit., "empty one"), how ugly you are. Are all your fellow citizens as ugly as you are?"
>
> The man replied: "I do not know, but go and tell the Craftsman who made me, 'How ugly is the vessel which You have made.'" When R. Eleazar realized that he had done wrong he dismounted from the donkey and prostrated himself before the man and said to him, "I submit myself to you, forgive me." The man replied, "I will not forgive you until you go to the Craftsman who made me and say to him, 'How ugly is the vessel which You have made.'"

He [R. Eleazar] walked behind him until he reached his native city. When his fellow citizens came out to meet him greeting him with the words, "Peace be upon you O teacher, O master." The man asked them, "Whom are you addressing thus?" They replied, "The man who is walking behind you." Thereupon he exclaimed, "If this man is a teacher, may there not be any more like him in Israel!" The people then asked him: "Why?" He replied, "Such and such a thing has he done to me."

They said to him: "Nevertheless, forgive him, for he is a man greatly learned in the Torah." The man replied, "For your sake I will forgive him, but only on the condition that he does not act in the same manner in the future." Soon after this, R. Eleazar son of R. Shimon entered [the study hall] and expounded thus, "A man should always be gentle as the reed and let him never be unyielding as the cedar." And for this reason the reed merited that of it should be made a pen for the writing of the Law, *tefillin* and *mezuzot* (*Taanit* 20a-b).

12. Seforno on Gen. 1:26 defines man's likeness to God as his endowment with free choice, which distinguishes man not only from other life forms on earth, but even heavenly creatures like angels, who must carry out whatever missions they may be assigned.

13. Man's potential superiority to the angels is based upon the difference between men and all other creatures with regard to free choice. Even if angels are always carrying out God's bidding, they do so because they have no alternative. When man does the right thing, he has chosen to do so, and this is a more profound indication of the Godliness of his nature than the actions of others who have been programmed to do the right thing.

14. Rabbi Akiva is also the person who teaches *chayecha kodmin* (see *Bava Metzia* 62a), which may serve as an upper bound of physical survival, even in accordance with Lev. 19:18. However, he continued to teach

Torah even when it was prohibited under threat of death, suggesting that when it comes to the spiritual survival of the Jewish people, there is no upper bound.

15. People commonly use themselves as their point of reference. This is also true in the talmudic passage which teaches that when someone finds fault in others, he is really finding fault in himself, conventionally stated in Hebrew as *kol ha-posel be-mumo posel* (see *Kiddushin* 70a, which does not use this exact phrasing).

16. An educational concept that assumes that since not everything can be taught or studied, certain choices will have to be made and priorities determined. Furthermore, whenever a certain subject or approach is chosen, it perforce will exclude certain alternate material due to limitations in time and attention span.

17. I would distinguish between accurate, factual accounts of great people's lives and hagiography. Revisionist works are suspect not only when disconnects are discovered between factual events and what is reported, but also when what is described appears to be "too good to be true."

18. Schocken Books, New York, 2006.

CHAPTER 3

PARING THE TORAH'S PRINCIPLES

תלמוד בבלי מסכת מכות דף כג עמוד ב — — כד עמוד א
דרש רבי שמלאי: שש מאות ושלש עשרה מצות נאמרו לו למשה, שלש מאות וששים וחמש לאוין כמנין ימות החמה, ומאתים וארבעים ושמונה עשה כנגד איבריו של אדם. אמר רב המנונא: מאי קרא? "תורה צוה לנו משה מורשה"—תורה בגימטריא שית מאה וחד סרי הוי, "אנכי" ו"לא יהיה לך" מפי הגבורה שמענום. (סימן: דמשמ"ק ס"ק). בא דוד והעמידן על אחת עשרה, דכתיב: "מזמור לדוד (ה') מי יגור באהלך מי ישכון בהר קדשך, הולך תמים ופועל צדק ודובר אמת בלבבו, לא רגל על לשונו לא עשה לרעהו רעה וחרפה לא נשא על קרובו, נבזה בעיניו נמאס ואת יראי ה' יכבד נשבע להרע ולא ימיר, כספו לא נתן בנשך ושוחד על נקי לא לקח עושה אלה לא ימוט לעולם". "הולך תמים—זה אברהם, דכתיב: "התהלך לפני והיה תמים". "פועל צדק"—כגון אבא חלקיהו. "ודובר אמת בלבבו"—כגון רב ספרא. "לא רגל על לשונו"—זה יעקב אבינו, דכתיב: "אולי ימושני אבי והייתי בעיניו כמתעתע". "לא עשה לרעהו רעה"—שלא ירד לאומנות חבירו. "וחרפה לא נשא על קרובו"—זה המקרב את קרוביו. "נבזה בעיניו נמאס"—זה חזקיהו המלך שגירר עצמות אביו במטה של חבלים. "ואת יראי ה' יכבד"—זה יהושפט מלך יהודה, שבשעה שהיה רואה תלמיד חכם, היה עומד מכסאו ומחבקו ומנשקו וקורא לו: (אבי אבי) רבי רבי, מרי מרי. "נשבע להרע ולא

ימיר"—כר' יוחנן, דא"ר יוחנן: אהא בתענית עד שאבא לביתי. "כספו לא נתן בנשך"—אפילו ברבית עובד כוכבים. "ושוחד על נקי לא לקח"—כגון ר' ישמעאל בר' יוסי. כתיב: "עושה אלה לא ימוט לעולם", כשהיה ר"ג מגיע למקרא הזה היה בוכה, אמר: מאן דעביד להו לכולהו הוא דלא ימוט, הא חדא מינייהו ימוט! אמרו ליה: מי כתיב "עושה כל אלה"? "עושה אלה" כתיב, אפילו בחדא מינייהו; דאי לא תימא הכי, כתיב קרא אחרינא: "אל תטמאו בכל אלה", התם נמי הנוגע בכל אלה הוא דמטמא, בחדא מינייהו לא? אלא לאו באחת מכל אלה, הכא נמי באחת מכל אלו. בא ישעיהו והעמידן על שש, דכתיב: "הולך צדקות ודובר מישרים מואס בבצע מעשקות נוער כפיו מתמוך בשוחד אוטם אזנו משמוע דמים ועוצם עיניו מראות ברע". "הולך צדקות"—זה אברהם אבינו, דכתיב: "כי ידעתיו למען אשר יצוה וגו'". "ודובר מישרים"—זה שאינו מקניט פני חבירו ברבים. "מואס בבצע מעשקות"—כגון ר' ישמעאל בן אלישע. "נוער כפיו מתמוך בשוחד"—כגון ר' ישמעאל בר' יוסי. "אוטם אזנו משמוע דמים"—דלא שמע בזילותא דצורבא מרבנן ושתיק, כגון ר"א ברבי שמעון. "ועוצם עיניו מראות ברע"—כדרבי חייא בר אבא, דאמר ר' חייא בר אבא: זה שאינו מסתכל בנשים בשעה שעומדות על הכביסה. וכתיב: "הוא מרומים ישכון (וגו')". בא מיכה והעמידן על שלש, דכתיב: "הגיד לך אדם מה טוב ומה ה' דורש ממך כי אם עשות משפט ואהבת חסד והצנע לכת עם (ה') אלקיך". "עשות משפט"— זה הדין. "אהבת חסד"—זה גמילות חסדים. "והצנע לכת"—זה הוצאת המת והכנסת כלה. והלא דברים קל וחומר: ומה דברים שאין דרכן לעשותן בצנעא—אמרה תורה: והצנע לכת, דברים שדרכן לעשותן בצנעא—על אחת כמה וכמה. חזר ישעיהו והעמידן על שתים, שנאמר: "כה אמר ה' שמרו משפט ועשו צדקה". בא עמוס והעמידן על אחת שנאמר: "כה אמר ה' לבית ישראל דרשוני וחיו". מתקיף לה רב נחמן בר יצחק, אימא: דרשוני בכל התורה כולה! אלא, בא חבקוק והעמידן על אחת, שנאמר: "וצדיק באמונתו יחיה".

The Great Principle of the Torah

Babylonian Talmud *Makkot* 23b-24a

R. Simlai when preaching said: Six hundred and thirteen precepts were communicated to Moses, three hundred and sixty-five negative precepts, corresponding to the number of solar days [in the year], and two hundred and forty-eight positive precepts, corresponding to the number of the members of man's body. Said R. Hamnuna: What is the text for this? It is, "Moses commanded us Torah, an inheritance of the congregation of Jacob" (Deut. 33:4). "*Torah*" being in letter-value equal to six hundred and eleven, "I Am" and "You shall have no [other gods]" [not counted because] we heard from the mouth of the mighty One.

David came and established them [the Torah's commandments] on eleven [principles], as it is written, "A Psalm of David. Lord, who shall sojourn in Your tabernacle? Who shall dwell in Your holy mountain? — (1) He that walks uprightly, and (2) does righteousness, and (3) speaks truth in his heart; that (4) has no slander upon his tongue, (5) nor does evil to his fellow, (6) nor takes up a reproach against his neighbor, (7) in whose eyes a vile person is despised, but (8) he honors them that fear the Lord, (9) He swears to his own hurt and changes not, (10) He puts not out his money on interest, (11) nor takes a bribe against the innocent. He that does these things shall never be moved" (Psalm 15).

"He that walks uprightly": that was Abraham, as it is written, "Walk before Me and be you whole-hearted" (Gen. 17:1). "And does righteousness," such as Abba Chilkia. "Speaks truth in his heart," such as R. Safra. "Has no slander upon his tongue," that was our father Jacob, as it is written, "My father might feel me and I shall seem to him as a deceiver" (Gen. 27:12). "Nor does evil to his fellow," that is he who does not set up in opposition to his fellow craftsman. "Nor takes up a reproach against his neighbor," that is he who befriends his near ones [relatives]. "In whose eyes a vile person is despised," that was Hezekiah the King [of Judah] who dragged his father's bones on a rope truckle-bed. "He honors them that fear the Lord," that was Jehoshaphat king of Judah, who every time he beheld a scholar-disciple rose from his throne, and embraced and kissed him, calling him "Father, Father, Rabbi, Rabbi, Master, Master!" "He swears to his own hurt and changes not," like R. Yochanan; for R. Yochanan [once] said, "I shall remain fasting until I reach home." "He puts not out money on interest," not even interest from a heathen. "Nor takes a bribe against the innocent," such as R. Yishmael son of R. Yosi. It is written [in conclusion], "He that does these things shall never be moved."

Whenever R. Gamaliel came to this passage he used to weep, saying: [Only] one who practiced all these shall not be moved; but anyone falling short in any of these [virtues] would be moved!

Said his colleagues to him: Is it written, "He that does *all* these things [shall not fall]" (Psalm 15:5)? It reads, "He that does these things," meaning even if only he practices one of these things [he shall not be moved]. For if you say otherwise, what of that other passage, "Defile not yourselves in all these things" (Lev. 18:24)? Are we to say that one who seeks contact with all these sources of impurity, he is become contaminated; but if only with one of those sources, he is not contaminated? [Surely] it can only mean there, that if he seeks contact with any one of these vices he is become contaminated, and likewise here, if he practices even one of these virtues [he will not be moved].

Isaiah came and established [the Torah's laws] on six [principles], as it is written, "(12) He that walks righteously, and (13) speaks uprightly, (14) He that despises the gain of oppressions, (15) that shakes his hand from holding of bribes, (16) that stops his ear from hearing of blood, (17) and shuts his eyes from looking upon evil; he shall dwell on High" (Isa. 33:15-16).

"He that walks righteously," that was our father Abraham, as it is written, "For I have known him, to the end that he may command his children and his household after him…" (Gen. 18:19); "and speaks uprightly," that is one who does not put an affront on his fellow in public. "He that despises the gain of oppressions," as, for instance, R. Yishmael b. Elisha; "that shakes his hand from holding of bribes," as, for instance, R. Yishmael son of Yosi; "that stops his ear from hearing of blood," one who hears not aspersions made against a rabbinic student and remains silent, as once did R. Eleazar son of R. Shimon; "and shuts his eyes from looking upon evil," as R. Chiya b. Abba [taught], for R. Chiya b. Abba said: This refers to one who does not peer at women as they stand washing clothes, and [concerning such a man] it is written, "He shall dwell on High."

Micah came and established them on three [principles], as it is written, "It has been told to you, O man, what is good, and what the Lord requires of you: (18) only to do justly, and (19) to love mercy and (20) to walk humbly before your God" (Micah 6:8).

"To do justly," that is, maintaining justice; "and to love mercy," that is, rendering every kind office; "and walking humbly before your God," that is, walking in funeral and bridal processions.

And do not these facts warrant an *a fortiori* conclusion that if in matters that are not generally performed in private the Torah enjoins "walking humbly," is it not ever so much more requisite in matters that usually call for modesty?

Again came Isaiah and established them on two [principles], as it is said, "Thus says the Lord, (21) keep justice and (22) do righteousness..." (Isa. 56:1).

Amos came and established them on one [principle], as it is said, "For so says the Lord unto the house of Israel, (23) seek Me and live" (Amos 5:4).

To this R. Nachman b. Yitzchak demurred, saying: [Might it not be taken as:] "Seek Me by observing the whole Torah and live"? —

But it is Habakkuk who came and established them on one [principle], as it is said, "(24) But the righteous shall live by his faith" (Habakkuk 2:4).

An Ideal Source for Contemplating the Torah's Fundamental Principles

We noted in Chapter 2 that when there is a give-and-take among disputants, it is possible to understand each point of view better. This is much more difficult to do when only a single point of view is offered. Consequently, if one would search for a single source devoted to trying to articulate the point, *Makkot* 23b-24a is ideal, since this passage attempts to determine the overall goal or goals of a life serving God by presenting a list of ever-narrowing hypotheses, culminating in a single verse, "the righteous shall live by his faith" (Habakkuk 2:4). The list suggests that elegance and simplicity is of the essence, reminiscent of the non-Jew's challenging Hillel to state for him the essence of Judaism while he stands on one foot. The progression of shorter and shorter lists in the verses also implies that the more telegraphic and laconic the rule, the better it is. Unfortunately, understanding this passage in light of its author is impossible, since the passage is anonymous and lacking any historical context.

A Summary of the Talmudic Passage
The discussion begins by noting the existence of 613 commandments in the Torah.[1] The text then utilizes a literary license where it imagines that a series of prophets, David, Isaiah, Micah, Amos and Habakkuk, formulate meta-principles that are either distillations of, prerequisites for, or desired outcomes resulting from the Torah's vast array of commandments. The text implies that unless an individual manifests these qualities and characteristics, even if he has resolutely engaged in trying to fulfill the Torah's commandments, he has missed the point.

Organizing the 24 Concepts
This passage has twenty-four principles: David has eleven, Isaiah six, Micah three, Isaiah another two, Amos one, and Habakkuk one. How should the elements contained in these lists of verses culled from entire books of prophecy be categorized? We cannot assume that any of the twenty-four fundamentals are innovations that were not previously part of Jewish tradition, since the role of

the prophets is not "to establish a [new] faith, but to command people to fulfill the Torah" (Maimonides, *Yesodei ha-Torah* 9:1).

Consequently, we must approach the statements of David, Isaiah, Micah, Amos, and Habakkuk as either reformulations of commandments already prescribed, or meta-principles derived from either groups of commandments, or all of commandments taken together. Particularly the contributions of Amos ("Seek Me and live") and Habakkuk ("But the righteous shall live by his faith") suggest concepts of incredible scope and therefore deserve special attention. We will consider each of these ideas individually, once we complete discussing the talmudic passage as a whole.

Subdividing the 24 Concepts: Commandments vs. Attitudes

While some of the twenty-four concepts can be associated with specific commandments, others appear to be articulations of general attitudes, temperaments, and virtues.

Examples of associating elements listed in *Makkot* with statements in the Torah include:

Principle in *Makkot*	Parallel Torah Verse
(2) works righteousness	And you shall do that which is right and good in the sight of the Lord (Deut. 6:18)
(18) Only to do justly (21) Keep justice (22) do righteousness	Justice, justice you shall pursue (Deut. 16:20)
(3) speaks truth in his heart	Keep you far from a false matter (Exod. 23:7)

(4) that has no slander upon his tongue	You shall not go up and down as a talebearer among your people (Lev. 19:16)
(9) He swears to his own hurt and changes not	or if any one swear clearly with his lips to do evil, or to do good, whatsoever it be that a man shall utter clearly with an oath, and it be hid from him; and, when he knows of it, be guilty in one of these things (Lev. 5:4)
(10) He puts not out his money on interest	You shall not lend upon interest to thy brother: interest of money, interest of victuals, interest of anything that is lent upon interest (Deut. 23:20)
(11) nor take a bribe against the innocent (15) that shakes his hand from holding of bribes }	You shall not wrest judgment; you shall not respect persons (by perverting justice); neither shall you take a gift; for a gift blinds the eyes of the wise, and perverts the words of the righteous (Deut. 16:19)
(16) that stops his ear from hearing of blood	You shall not utter/accept a false report; put not your hand with the wicked to be an unrighteous witness (Exod. 23:1)
(17) and shuts his eyes from looking upon evil	neither shall you stand idly by the blood of your neighbor (Lev. 19:16)

Paring the Torah's Principles

The remainder of the twenty-four principles represents temperaments, but do not directly correspond with a verse from the Torah.

Interpersonal, Introspective (Personal), and Ritual Principles
Furthermore, the diverse elements listed in *Makkot* can be divided into thirteen qualities that are personal or introspective (*bein adam le-atzmo*), eight that are interpersonal (*bein adam le-chaveiro*), and three between man and God (*bein adam la-Makom*).

The thirteen introspective or personal (*bein adam le-atzmo*) are:

- "He that walks uprightly" (1);
- "works righteousness" (2);
- "speaks truth in his heart" (3);
- "has no slander upon his tongue" (4);
- "He swears to his own hurt and changes not" (9);
- "He that walks righteously" (12);
- "speaks uprightly" (13);
- "He that despises the gain of oppressions" (14);
- "shuts his eyes from looking upon evil; he shall dwell on High" (17);
- "Only to do justly" (18);
- "to love mercy"(19);
- "Keep justice" (21);
- "do righteousness" (22).

The eight interpersonal (*bein adam le-chaveiro*) are:

- "Nor does evil to his fellow" (5);
- "Nor takes up a reproach against his neighbor" (6);

- "In whose eyes a vile person is despised" (7);
- "He honors them that fear the Lord" (8);
- "He puts not out his money on interest" (10);
- "Nor takes a bribe against the innocent" (11);
- "That shakes his hand from holding of bribes" (15);
- "That stops his ear from hearing of blood" (16).

The three that are between man and God (*bein adam la-Makom*) are:

- "To walk humbly before thy God" (20)
- "For so says the Lord unto the house of Israel, seek Me and live" (23)
- "But the righteous shall live by his faith" (24).

Simply looking at the quantities of entries in each category, it could be argued that interpersonal commandments (*bein adam le-chaveiro*) are more important than commandments between man and God (*bein adam la-Makom*), a ratification of Hillel and Rabbi Akiva (Chapter 1) as well as Ben Azzai according to *Korban ha-Edah*, in contradistinction to Ben Azzai according to *Pnei Moshe* (Chapter 2). But then one also has to recognize that introspective commandments (*bein adam le-atzmo*) have the largest category of all. An approach that might account for this breakdown would maintain that if a person reaches a proper level of understanding and behavior regarding himself, positive activities regarding his fellow man and God become far more attainable.

From a qualitative perspective, one can readily recognize the difference between the last two teachings ("Seek Me and live" [23]; and "the righteous shall live by his faith" [24]), and the preceding twenty-two principles. These latter two are far more likely to include the twenty-two previous elements, while the opposite is not the case. I would posit that if a person is truly Godly, which according to some authorities is the goal of a religious quest, then perforce he must be kind and considerate to other human beings. The converse of this, however, is not necessarily the case; just because an individual is empathic to others, that does not mean that he believes in God or leads a religious lifestyle.[2]

Bein Adam le-Atzmo as a Rationale

The preponderance of concepts on this list has as its rationale introspective commandments (*bein adam le-atzmo*). This finds supports in the evocative words of Maimonides:

> All of these ordinances are to subjugate one's evil inclination and improve one's character. Similarly, most of the Torah's laws are nothing other than "counsels given from distance" from "He Who is of great counsel" (1) to improve one's character and (2) to make one's conduct upright.[3] And so it is written, "Behold, I have written for you in the Torah prominent matters, to inform you of the veracity of the words of truth, so that you will respond truthfully to those who I send to you" (*Temurah* 4:13, quoting Prov. 22:20-21).[4]

Yet it is important to note a fundamental difference between the examples found in *Makkot*, on the one hand, and Maimonides' rule, on the other: in the case of the former, for the most part,[5] very specific activities and attitudes are listed, in contrast to the vastly more general and imprecise two principles appearing in *Mishneh*

Torah. "Improving one's character" and "making one's conduct upright" are far less specific than, for example, not engaging in slander, not charging interest, or carefully carrying out one's oaths.

Maimonides' general principles are not clearly defined, allowing a wide range of opinions about how personality improvement can best be undertaken. In contrast, the specificity of most of the twenty-four elements in *Makkot* 23b-24a leaves far less to the imagination and requires very specific behaviors. Yet as the list of elements becomes shorter and broader, inevitably, we run into the same problem of detail versus essence. Establishing the proper balance between these two types of articulation is challenging within any context.

"He Established Them" (*Ve-He'emidan*)

Perhaps the key component in this passage in *Makkot* that reveals the relationship between these twenty-four actions and attitudes on the one hand, and the actual commandments of the Torah on the other, is the word *ve-he'emidan* ("he established them," lit., "and caused them to stand"), which is used six times. The Soncino edition translates the first five usages as "reduced them," and the final *ve-he'emidan* as "based them all," when quoting Habakkuk. The Soncino translation suggests that the 613 commandments can be *replaced* by the prophetic sources—instead of 613 commandments, it is acceptable to substitute a lesser number in their place.

Rashi's Approach: Reducibility

The Soncino translation of *ve-he'emidan* as "reduced them" is in accordance with Rashi's interpretation:

Initially, the people were righteous and they were able to accept the yoke of a great many commandments. But later generations were not as righteous, and if they would have to observe all of them, there would not be a single person who would be considered meritorious. "David came *ve-he'emidan*," in order that they will be meritorious if they fulfill these eleven commandments. And so it was in every time, that succeeding generations proceeded to diminish it[6] (Rashi, s.v., *ve-he'emidan al achat esreh*).

Rashi suggests that in accordance with the ubiquitous rabbinic principle *nitma'atu ha-dorot*, ("the ensuing generations were increasingly deficient"), the leaders of subsequent generations saw fit to progressively lower the bar of minimum observance so a life of Torah and *mitzvot* would not become the province of only a small elite.

The talmudic discussion suggests a further lowering of the bar:

Whenever R. Gamaliel came to this passage he used to weep, saying: [Only] one who practiced all these [eleven principles] shall not be moved; but anyone falling short in any of these [virtues] would be moved!

Said his colleagues to him: Is it written, "He that does *all* these things [shall not fall]"? It reads, "He that does *these things*" (Psalm 15:5), meaning even if only he practices one of these things [he shall not be moved]. For if you say otherwise, what of that other passage, "Defile not yourselves in *all* these things" (Lev. 18:24)? Are we to say that one who seeks contact with all these vices [i.e., *all* forms of sexual misconduct], he is become contaminated;

but if only with one of those vices, he is not contaminated? [Surely,] it can only mean there, that if he seeks contact with any one of these vices he is become contaminated, and likewise here, if he practices even one of these virtues [he will not be moved].

In other words, not only is having to comply with all 613 commandments deemed too daunting a task, but even having to comply with David's eleven principles will prove impossible for the average person, and in the end, carrying out a single one of them should be sufficient. In effect, at least quantitatively, there needs to be a single concept upon which people should be able to concentrate; the standard represented by Amos and Habakkuk's single verses is already anticipated by David, and by implication, by Isaiah and Micah as well.

It would appear that Rashi's approach is problematic for several reasons. First, even if the quantity of principles contracts over time, the content of these behaviors remains challenging and rigorous. Being able to act consistently in accordance with broad concepts like righteousness, justice, truth, humility, and faith is not a concession to spiritual weakness, but constitutes aspirational standards that should coexist with, if not even transcend, the 613 commandments.

Second, a methodological problem is raised by the commentary *Einei Yitzchak* (Rabbi Yitzchak Aharon ben Yehudah Leiv Dvilkamir, grandson of *Tosafot Yom Tov*, and author of commentary on *Ein Yaakov*), among others:

> And behold, the passage according to its simple meaning shocks the onlooker, because there is an explicit verse,

"You shall not add unto the word which I command you, neither shall you diminish from it, that you may keep the commandments of the Lord your God which I command you" (Deut. 4:2). So how could David reduce all 613 commandments into only eleven? And Isaiah into six, etc.? And commentators have already struggled with this question....[7]

Maimonides said that prophets cannot establish new laws (*Yesodei ha-Torah* 9:1, quoted above). How then can these same prophets legitimize the ignoring of a majority of the commandments?[8]

Maimonides' Approach: Specialization
Maimonides' approach is diametrically opposed to Rashi's opinion. Maimonides understands *ve-he'emidan* as referring to focus and concentration rather than merely replacement. Not only does the whole of the 613 commandments have an organic and unalterable reality, but according to one Tanna the extensive number of commandments is to give the Jewish people additional opportunities for merit.

> R. Chanania b. Akashia says: The Holy One, Blessed be He, desired to make Israel meritorious. Therefore He gave them the Torah [to study] and commandments [to perform]. As it is said, "The Lord was pleased for his [Israel's] righteousness' sake to make the Law great and glorious" (Mishnah, *Makkot* 3:16, quoting Isa. 42:21).

And while having more commandments to perform simultaneously creates the possibility of more violations, Maimonides offers another way to look at it:

> It is one of the fundamental principles of Jewish belief that if a person fulfills one of the 613 commandments appropriately and properly without attaching to it any of the ulterior motives associated with this world, but rather he performs it for its own sake [*lishmah*] with love, as I have explained to you,[9] behold he merits by means of it life in the World to Come. For this reason R. Chanania said that due to the multiplicity of commandments it is impossible that a person does not carry out [at least] one over the course of his lifetime in a perfect manner, and thereby merits the eternity of the soul by virtue of that action... (Maimonides, Commentary to *Makkot* 3:16).

In effect, according to Maimonides, Rashi's interpretation that the prophets reduced the number of commandments would make it more difficult for a Jew to earn the merit that God wishes him to attain. There would be fewer opportunities to fulfill one of the prophets' principles flawlessly. Maimonides is not suggesting that one single *mitzvah* ought to replace the others; rather he advocates that while an individual should strive to do all of the commandments, it is likely there is one he will excel at, and for this reason he will be acknowledged and rewarded. For Maimonides, *Makkot* 23b-24a is emphasizing such areas of specialization.

The Maharsha's Approach: Unity of the 613 Commandments
The Maharsha (Rabbi Samuel Eidels, 1555-1631) says that he sides with Maimonides, but then offers his own unique formulation, which defines the passage in *Makkot* as an exercise in differing frames of reference:

Paring the Torah's Principles

The Holy One, Blessed be He, gave us 613 commandments, 365 negative commandments and 248 positive commandments. And the multiplicity is due to the receiver [man], because from the perspective of the Giver, Blessed be He, all of them are like a single commandment. This is what is meant when the Talmud states, "'I Am' and 'You shall have no [other gods]' [not being reckoned among the 611, because] we heard from the mouth of the mighty One" (*Makkot* 23b). And they said in the Midrash: All the words [in the Ten Commandments] were spoken by God. So what is being taught with respect to "'I Am' and 'You shall have no [other gods]'"? It is to teach that God spoke the Ten Commandments in one utterance, something that is impossible for human beings to do. And it is understandable because He is One and His commandments are one, and multiplicity is not acceptable from His reality, blessed be He. And it is because with respect to the commandments, in the commandment "I Am" which is the belief in God's Oneness, and its opposite, "You shall have no [other gods]," i.e., not to partner the Name of Heaven with anything else, are included all the negative and positive commandments. But it is impossible for human beings to express themselves in this manner because man is a material being existing under the rubric of time, so multiplicity perforce must be part of his perspective. Therefore they said all of the commandments of the Torah are included in the Ten Commandments, as states Rabbi Saadiah. In the end all of the commandments are included in the commandment of belief which is the root and source for all of them.[10]

According to the Maharsha's interpretation of *ve-he'emidan*, the prophets progressively communicated to man how God views the entirety of the 613 commandments as a collective. The distillations of David, Isaiah, Micah, Amos, and Habakkuk communicate what God is "thinking," so to speak. These prophets teach us that when there is a disconnect between how we view our performance of the commandments, and God's expectations for us, it is important to bring our own perspective in line with God's expectations.

Based on this, one might wonder why it is important for man to gain understanding of God's view of the commandments. Will this in some way enhance man's sense of holiness and inspiration while performing the commandments which he is required to do? In other words, can the commandments only positively influence people when they recognize that the commandments are beneficial to their character development, or does it happen automatically?

ArtScroll's Approach: Ethical Underpinnings

ArtScroll's translation/interpretation[11] of *ve-he'emidan* avoids the difficulties in the Soncino version, as well as the theological conception of the Maharsha:

> King David came and established eleven ethical and moral requirements as the basis for the fulfillment of the 613 commandments.... Subsequent prophets felt it necessary to further reduce the number of basic ethical requirements that one must strive to master as a basis for fulfillment of all 613 commandments. Isaiah came and established the basis for fulfillment of the commandments of the Torah upon six ethical requirements.... Later it was necessary to reduce the number of ethical requirements

Paring the Torah's Principles

even further. The prophet Micah came and established the basis for fulfillment of the Torah's commandments upon three ethical requirements.... As Torah observance further deteriorated among the populace, the prophets reduced the number of ethical requirements even more. Isaiah again came and established the basis for the fulfillment of the Torah's commandments on two ethical requirements.... The prophet Amos came and established the basis for fulfilling the Torah's commandments upon one ethical requirement.... Rather it was the prophet Habakkuk who came and established them on the basis of one ethical requirement....

ArtScroll notes in a footnote, "This passage obviously does not mean that the commandments were gradually discarded in favor of the increasingly shorter lists given by the various prophets. Such a notion is impossible since the commandments of the Torah are eternal."

The implication of ArtScroll's translation of *ve-he'emidan* seems to me to come closest to responding to the problem addressed in this book—what is the irreducible essential ethic of the commandments? We are not looking to eliminate commandments, or seeking an esoteric, mystical understanding that comes closer to God's perspective, or even the desired outcome after all of the commandments have been performed. Rather, we are searching for an overall context, i.e., either the prerequisites for, or a set of Divine expectations that are meant to be worked on and realized while simultaneously performing the commandments themselves.

These prophetic-talmudic lists offer a means for evaluating whether a life of Torah and *mitzvot* can be meaningful and is having the desired effect. The twenty-four elements can be understood as an evaluative rubric to determine whether a person is on the correct path or not, and whether it is reasonable to assume that the *mitzvot* are having a positive effect upon their practitioners.

Are All 24 Qualities Necessary?
Let us now turn to the specific elements that the prophets propose would constitute the characteristics by which God wishes His chosen people to be distinguished as they adhere to His commandments.

David gave a list of eleven qualities, eight of which are augmented in the Talmud by specific people or behaviors.[12] Some traits are illustrated in *Makkot* by specific individuals drawn from various periods in Jewish history,[13] or examples of particular behaviors that exemplify each of these qualities:

No.	Quality	Personality	Prooftext
1	He that walks uprightly	Abraham	"Walk before Me and be wholehearted" (Gen. 17:1).
2	And works	Abba Chilkiahu	(see *Taanit* 23a-b).
3	Speaks truth in his heart	R. Safra	He was reciting the *Shema,* and a man said to him, "Sell me your wares for so and so much money." And he [the purchaser] thought that because his offer was too little, he [R. Safra] did not respond [because he was praying]. And he [the purchaser] offered him a much greater sum. After his prayer, he [R. Safra] refused to accept any amount other than the original offer since he had decided in his heart to sell to him for that sum... (Rashbam to *Bava Batra* 88a, s.v., *R. Safra*).

4	Has no slander on his tongue	Jacob	"My father might feel me and I shall seem to him as a deceiver" (Gen. 27:12).
5	Nor does evil to his fellow	one who does not set up opposition to his fellow craftsman	-
6	Nor takes up a reproach against his neighbor	one who befriends his relatives	-
7	In whose eyes a vile person is despised	Hezekiah, who dragged his father's bones on a rope truckle-bed	-
8	He who honors them that fears the Lord	Jehoshaphat, who every time he beheld a scholar-disciple rose from his throne, and embraced and kissed him, calling him "Father, Father, Rabbi, Rabbi, Master, Master!"	-

9	He swears to his own hurt and changes not	Rabbi Yochanan	Rabbi Yochanan said, "I will remain fasting until I reach home." *Taanit* 12a says this was to avoid eating in the house of the Nasi.
10	He puts not out money on interest	not even from a heathen	-
11	Nor takes a bribe against the innocent	Rabbi Ishmael b. Rav Yosi	See *Ketubot* 105b.

An interesting difference in understanding arises when we first look at Psalm 15 without the benefit of the Talmud's explanation and without examples of each of the qualities, and only then consider *Makkot*'s exposition of these attitudes and practices.

We can accept the assumption that the qualities mentioned in David's list constitute the standard moral, ethical, and spiritual characteristics expected of all those who aspire to lead a life of Torah and *mitzvot*, since the Psalm opens with the words, "A Psalm of David. Lord, who shall sojourn in Your tabernacle? Who shall dwell upon Your holy mountain?" (Psalm 15:1). As Malbim explains, these phrases refer to those who are worthy to stand before God, not just the most exceptional religious personalities, but rather all those who attempt to live in accordance with Torah and *mitzvot*.

These qualities are relatively reasonable and accessible to everyone. Yet when we turn to most of the specific examples provided in the Talmud, the elements in the list are viewed as *middot chasidut* (attributes of exceptional piety) or applications of the principle *lifnim mi-shurat ha-din* (going beyond the letter of the law) and applicable only to a very select few. For example, how many individuals truly have the capacity to reach the high level of ethical and spiritual development implied by the verse "Walk before Me and be whole-hearted"? Is it reasonable to assume that the average Jew should be willing and able to publicly disparage a parent who had engaged in reprehensible activity as did Hezekiah? And is it typical to define bribes not only as tangible gifts, but even as subtle favors, powerfully modeled by Rabbi Ishmael b. Rav Yosi?

The List's Aspirational Purpose

One helpful frame of reference for better understanding the relationship between David's list and the Talmud's specific examples, is indirectly mentioned by Rabbi Aharon Lichtenstein[14] in an essay that speaks at length about the halakhic concept of *lifnim mi-shurat ha-din* (going beyond the letter of the law). He cites Lon Fuller's[15] evocative idea that one must distinguish between the "morality of duty" and the "morality of aspiration." Rabbi Lichtenstein posits that we must recognize that "a Jew is also commanded to aspire."[16] Consequently, while the examples appearing in *Makkot* 23b-24a are reflective of maximal applications of David's principles, and all Jews would do well to aspire to such attitudes and behavior, nevertheless these examples do not contradict the need for minimal compliance (which is also laudatory). By defining the ideal in terms of rarified examples, the Talmud challenges man to continue to strive over the course of his lifetime and to never assume that he has achieved all that is possible. Much of Jewish ethics is based upon not only the examples of our sages and holy men, but by God setting for man an example of ethical behavior.

It is impossible for any person to ever conduct himself exactly like God, but nevertheless man is expected, on his own level, to strive to emulate God and walk in His ways.[17] The same could be said about the extraordinary human examples that *Makkot* lists to illustrate David's eleven ethical and spiritual concepts. What is important is to emulate these behaviors and attitudes on whatever level one is able, constantly improving, even as one diligently studies Torah and performs the *mitzvot*.

Realistic and Idealistic Goals

A second, somewhat parallel, approach is suggested by Nechama Leibowitz in her worksheet for *Parashat Ki Teitzei* 5728,[18] in the section entitled *Alon ha-Derakhah* (Instructional Guide). Regarding the commandment of *hashavat aveidah* (returning a lost object),[19] Nechama (as she preferred to be called) gives the following directive to teachers who will be presenting this material to their classes:

> One should clarify from the start that we are not dealing with the return of lost objects in the sense of moral instruction, but rather that this an actual positive commandment—therefore the *mitzvah* is defined and limited so that it is not behavior with which the majority of the community cannot comply. Consequently we do not require the finder of the lost object to lose financially on behalf of another,[20] nor is he required to do anything on behalf of the object that he has found that he would not do

for his own property. It is sufficient that he demonstrates concern for the possessions of another comparable to how he relates to his own possessions.

In other words, Nechama posits that Jewish tradition presents desired behavior in at least two different forms. When our primary sources deal with requirements that apply to everyone, the expectations regarding desired behavior will be more average than idealistic. It is only when the Written and Oral Traditions discuss ideals towards which one should strive, in Nechama's words, *hatafat musar* (preaching ethical directives), that we are presented with singular examples of the spiritual elite. Applying this assumption to *Makkot* 23b-24a leads to the understanding that the Talmud views the prophets as giving *musar* to the listeners, and therefore most examples are radical and atypical.

David and Isaiah's List Compared
Looking beyond these problems, it is possible to generalize David's list as focusing upon four elements: (1) honesty (principles 3, 9); (2) integrity (principle 8); (3) morality (principles 1, 2, 8, 10); and (4) goodness (principles 4, 5, 6, 11).

The subsequent lists clearly differ in terms of quantity. Yet do they also differ with respect to quality? In other words, which of the four essential areas of human conduct addressed by David are eliminated, and which, if any, are added in the subsequent lists? Let us first compare David and Isaiah's lists along with the Talmud's examples. A cursory comparison indicates that all of Isaiah's examples parallel something cited by David:[21]

David	Isaiah
He that walks uprightly (1)	walks uprightly (13)
works righteousness (2)	He that walks righteously (12)
has no slander on his tongue (4)	stops his ear from hearing of blood (16)
nor does evil to his fellow (5)	despises the gain of oppression (14)
in whose eyes a vile person is despised (7)	shuts his eyes from looking upon evil (17)
nor takes a bribe against the innocent (11)	shakes his hand from holding bribes (15)

Of the four categories in David's list (honesty, integrity, morality, and goodness), the quality of honesty is absent from Isaiah's list. Perhaps in the interests of condensation, integrity was thought to include honesty within its purview.

There are two commonalities in the Talmud's explication of the lists of David and Isaiah. First, both lists reference Abraham as an exemplar of uprightness and righteousness. Second, Rabbi Ishmael b. Rav Yosi is identified as refusing to take bribes. This in turn draws attention to the story of R. Ishmael b. Elisha who despised illegal gains. These stories appear in a series of six anecdotes in *Ketubot* 105b, all intended to exemplify subtle forms of bribery that outstanding individuals avoided. Why should *Makkot* 24a feel a need to connect two of Isaiah's six elements to demonstrate the same concept—the extent to which bribery ought to be avoided? Furthermore all of the anecdotes in *Ketubot* 105b are dealing with Rabbis who served as judges in disputes between Jews, and who recused themselves due to the possibility of bias. Yet there is an extremely small number of candidates who are qualified judges. However, the lists of David and Isaiah delineate moral and spiritual principles applicable to all Jews. Perforce it must be concluded that the warning against bribery applies not only to judges, but to all people in various everyday situations. The need for objectivity, even in non-legal contexts, is apparently considered by *Makkot* 24a as a meta-principle that is worth emphasizing more than once even in the short list of six qualities connected to Isaiah.

When the lists of David and Isaiah are considered together, it can be concluded that according to *Makkot* 24a, the way one treats others is of paramount importance to religious life. The manner in which an individual carries himself, works, speaks, and avoids or reacts to evil, defines whether or not a Jew is being true to his tradition.

Micah's List

The Talmud in *Makkot* then cites still shorter prophetic lists[22] of essential qualities, the first two appearing to make the same points as David and Isaiah, but in more concentrated form. A list of three elements is attributed to the prophet Micah: "only to do justly (18), and to love mercy (19), and to walk humbly before thy God (20)" (Micah 6:8).

While David and Isaiah's lists were supported by the actions of specific people, Micah's list is supplemented by general types of behavior, described impersonally:

> "To do justly," that is, maintaining justice; "and to love mercy," that is, rendering every kind office; "and walking humbly before your God," that is, walking in funeral and bridal processions.

The Great Principle of the Torah

Micah's formulation is as follows:

- "To do justly," that is, maintaining justice [the ideal is to consistently engage in just acts over time];
- "and to love mercy," that is, rendering every kind office [kindness must be an informing principle in virtually everything that one does];
- "and walking humbly before thy God," that is, walking in funeral and bridal processions [even when walking in public display one should walk with humility].

The only novel element that emerges from Micah's list is the mention of humility. Although David and Isaiah did not mention humility, since Abraham is an exemplar in both cases, that establishes a clear connection. Abraham demonstrated his humility when pleading for Sodom and Gomorrah, "And Abraham answered and said: 'Behold now, I have taken upon me to speak unto the Lord, who am but dust and ashes'" (Gen. 18:27).[23]

It is interesting that the Talmud's explication of "walking humbly" addresses two contexts with which we do not normally associate humility—funeral and wedding processions. The purpose of participating in funerals is to honor the deceased as well as the survivors,[24] while the prime objective when attending a wedding is to cause the bride and groom to rejoice.[25] Each of these communal experiences includes a procession: accompanying the remains to the place of burial, and, according to the Talmud, the escorting of the celebrants from their parental homes to the place where the wedding is to take place.[26] The aspect of modesty arises because the participant should not make it about himself when the focus should so obviously be on the celebrants at a wedding, or mourners at a funeral.

By extension, humility should not be practiced only at public events, but also in private life. One might think it only applies in social situations, where one's behavior would be noticed by others. But when we realize we are always standing before God, we recognize that all of our actions, whether in public or private, should be done with humility.

Isaiah's Second List
Makkot 24a next cites a different verse in Isaiah, which instead of six qualities, advocates only two, without the Talmud explicating them any further: "Keep ye justice (21), and do righteousness (22)" (Isa. 56:8).

In Micah's list and Isaiah's second list, the number of elements is reduced by omitting actions to be avoided; everything is stated positively. Furthermore, the language these prophets use, with the notable exception of Micah's emphasis on the value of acting mercifully, calls to mind the specific verses that have been associated with Abraham in the earlier lists:

Abraham	Micah	Isaiah
Walk before Me (Gen. 17:1)	Walk humbly before your God (Micah 6:8)	-
and be whole-hearted (Gen. 17:1)	-	-
For I have known him, to the end that he may command his children and his household after him, that they may keep the way of the Lord, *to do righteousness...* (Gen. 18:19)	-	Do righteousness (Isa. 56:1)

... and keep justice (Gen. 18:19)	only to do justice (Micah 6:8)	... keep ye justice (56:1)
-	and to love mercy (Micah 6:8)	-

It is possible that the negative is implied in the positive formulation.[27] For example, walking before God means avoiding things that are unsuitable before God. Similarly, acting righteously also means avoiding unrighteous action; and pursuing justice means rejecting injustice. As the lists become increasingly concentrated, the emphasis is placed upon acting positively towards others and being inspired by God to do so.

Amos and Habakkuk

Finally, we are taught two formulations in which a single element is deemed sufficient to serve as the key to religious growth and perfection. In both instances, it would appear that a marked change from what has been previously cited informs these last prophetic pronouncements:

> Amos: "For thus says the Lord unto the house of Israel, seek Me and live" (Amos 5:4).

> Habakkuk: "But the righteous shall live by his faith" (Habakkuk 2:4).

In these last two prophetic statements, the focus has shifted. Instead of exemplary interpersonal behavior, the focal point has become the way one relates to God. As we have indicated earlier, interpersonal and God-oriented commandments are not necessarily complementary. Consequently, one might wonder whether this shift in emphasis encourages an individual to concentrate upon ritual law and theological studies at the expense of a high level of standards relating to one's fellow man.

The medieval commentator Meiri (1249-c. 1310) deconstructs Habakkuk's statement in a manner that does not allow for someone to use Amos or Habakkuk to justify being derelict in his interpersonal obligations:

> All commandments have a single purpose, and it is the goal towards which every reflective individual should direct all of his activities, and that is the intention to serve God, and this is what is meant when they said, "All of your actions should be for the sake of Heaven" (*Betzah* 16a). And this is what is being interpreted here regarding all commandments, "But it is Habakkuk who came and based them all on one [principle], as it is said, "But the righteous shall live by his faith" (Habakkuk 2:4).

The Meiri suggests that Habakkuk is not promoting one group of commandments over another, but rather is stressing that all commandments, whether between man and God or between man and man, should be viewed as different forms of Divine service. In that regard, Habakkuk negates all sorts of ulterior motives in favor of a purified approach to Torah and *mitzvot*. Not only can ulterior motives adversely affect *mitzvot* between man and God, but there are many imperfect intentions that can accompany interpersonal behavior. When all of one's actions are truly "for the sake of Heaven," this means that the individual has properly internalized the words of the Torah and its values.[28]

Although Habakkuk appears to have the last word, Rabbi Nachman bar Yitzchak's rejection of Amos' verse does not appear absolute. Perhaps "seek Me and live" can be interpreted as "fulfill *all* the commandments of the Torah and live." Why does this delegitimize the centrality of Amos' teaching? The spirit of the inquiry in this talmudic passage is to narrow the list of attributes in order to illustrate the point of Judaism. The fact that Amos 5:4 might achieve just the opposite, i.e., reinstate all commandments as the optimal goal, while true, does not fulfill to purpose of trying to narrow things down, and once again obscures the identity of the meta-principle being sought.

If this is what Amos meant, then Amos and Habakkuk emphasize very different aspects of an individual's relationship with God. Habakkuk's verse, addressing the conception that faith in God informs a righteous person's life, suggests a condition of stasis. The verse implies that one does not necessarily grow or develop in *emunah* (belief, faith); it is a state of mind that determines one's actions and attitudes. Alternatively, Amos' verse describes a never-ending journey and quest to achieve deeper understanding and appreciation of God. Habakkuk's verse describes how a righteous individual functions at any given point, whereas the former encompasses someone's totality of religious experience—one that is dynamic and in constant flux. Naturally, R. Nachman bar Yitzchak's objection cannot be discounted, but I view the verses of Amos and Habakkuk as complementary descriptions of a life in which faith plays a central role.

Implications for Contemporary Jews

A number of insights arise from reading and analyzing *Makkot* 23b-24a. While within the immediate context of prophetic writings, one can reflect upon the situation that inspired the prophet to remonstrate the people in the manner that he does, the Talmud approaches these texts as if they are setting standards for ourselves in the present day and therefore have enduring applicability.

The Rabbis teach that there were many prophets, but their prophecies were only recorded if their teachings were required for future generations.[29]

Consequently, the contemporary reader should consider the words of David, Isaiah, Micah, Amos, and Habakkuk as being directed to him personally, and take those teachings to heart. The passage in *Makkot* presents these prophecies on a grander scale, looking for parallels and essences. But the messages from all of the prophets are pertinent and should be internalized as much as possible.

Furthermore, the preponderance of the statements in *Makkot* addresses excellence in interpersonal behavior. This means that every person serious about Judaism must devote significant time on an ongoing basis to study material like *Musar*—works intended to promote emotional intelligence, and theories of morals and ethics, and then reflect upon how to internalize these ideas and act upon them.

Another issue highlighted by these discussions is the tension between what is a reasonable minimum standard, in contrast to the goals and ideals to which we should constantly aspire. Particularly in light of the Meiri, who casts all commandments, even interpersonal ones, as examples of Divine service, to what extent should one push himself to realize the ideal of Judaism?

With respect to the virtue of humility, which appears on only one list, to what extent are people able to hone this trait? Is humility a quality that can be refined, developed, and enhanced to the same extent as other virtues mentioned by the prophets? If yes, how can an individual strive to become more humble, without harming his self-image and self-esteem?

If Maharsha is correct that all of the commandments are complementary, to what extent must someone integrate all of the commandments (introspective, interpersonal, and ritual alike) to achieve *shleimut* (wholeness)?

Finally, Amos and Habakkuk's emphasis on faith clearly defines the importance of "God-think" and "God-talk," i.e., devoting time to directly and unabashedly thinking about and articulating how each of us feels about our relationship to the Divine. Instead of avoiding such a topic because it appears too esoteric, we should devote more time to such reflection and discussion to enhance our ability to aspire to incorporate God's attributes into our own personalities and practices.

Paring the Torah's Principles

Endnotes

1. Rabbi Simlai derives the number 613 as a homiletic interpretation of the number of commandments that are in the Torah. He derives it using *gematria* (Hebrew numerology), where the Hebrew word תורה is equal to 611. He then quotes the verse, "Moses commanded us the Torah" (Deut. 33:4); Moses commanded us all but the first two of the Ten Commandments, which were spoken directly by God (since those are written in first person), "*I* am the Lord your God," and "You shall have no other gods beside *Me*." Hence Rabbi Simlai's conclusion of 613.

The actual number of commandments is many more than 613, and when combined with commandments legislated by the Rabbis as well as customs that have taken on the status of Jewish law, the total number of mandated activities for traditional Jews numbers in the thousands. See Maimonides' introduction to *Sefer ha-Mitzvot* for a means by which the number of commandments can be narrowed down to 613.

2. The talmudic passage quoted in Chapter Two discusses someone who excels in interpersonal commandments but is deficient in his obligations to God, or excels in ritual commandments but falls short in interpersonal matters (*Kiddushin* 40a).

3. Rabbi Natan Slifkin, in a blog posting "Rationalist Judaism" says that for many Rishonim, all commandments serve one or more of three purposes: (a) teaching us concepts, (b) improving our characters and (c) improving society. http://www.rationalistjudaism.com/2014/06/the-function-of-prayer-and-tehillim.html

4. A similar comment by Maimonides in the *Mishneh Torah* concerns the basis of the commandments:

> It is forbidden to hesitate before transgressing the Sabbath [laws] on behalf of a person who is dangerously ill, as it says,

"which a person shall perform to live through them" (Lev. 18:5), as "to live through them' and not to die through them" (*Yoma* 85b). This teaches that the judgments of the Torah [1] do not [bring] vengeance to the world, but rather [2] bring mercy, [3] kindness, and [4] peace to the world… (*Hilkhot Shabbat* 2:3).

The question that this citation raises is whether the four values that Maimonides claims underlie the commandments will be internalized merely by performing them, or does the individual have to consciously be aware of these values in order for them to have any effect.

5. Of the twenty-four elements in the various lists, in my view only the following four could be said to be far more general than specific: "He that walks uprightly" (1), "he that walks righteously" (12), "speaks uprightly" (13), "to walk humbly before thy God" (20). And yet even these four are more specific than Maimonides' very general terminology: "improving one's character" and "making one's conduct upright."

6. Rashi's assumption is that because people were not adhering to the Torah, the minimum standards needed to be adjusted downwards. This is curious. Why is he reluctant to state that there no longer are virtuous people, as compared to past generations? This can be compared to what Rashi says about Noah and his generation: "Noah was a righteous man, blameless in his generation" (Gen. 6:9). Rashi writes, "There are some of our Rabbis who see this phrase as praise to him, [if he could be righteous in a generation of sinners, he would have been] all the more so had he lived in a generation of righteous individuals. And there are those who interpret it as a denigration, i.e., regarding his generation he was righteous, but had he lived during the generation of Abraham, he would not have been considered worthy in the least way" (s.v., *be-dorotav*, quoting *Sanhedrin* 109).

But Rashi in *Makkot* provides no such qualifier. Rather, because there was a decrease in the level of observance, the quantity of commandments by which an individual's virtue was to be measured, was reduced.

7. See, e.g., the beginning of Maharsha's comments on *Makkot* 23b, s.v., *taryag mitzvot ne'emru Le-Mosheh*.

8. It is possible the prophets were reducing them as a *hora'at sha'ah* (temporary measure). See Chapter 4.

9. See Maimonides' commentary to *Sanhedrin* 10:1.

10. Maharsha, s.v. *u-va David ve-he'emidan*. Maharsha's conception that from God's viewpoint, there should be fewer rather than more commandments, parallels an understanding that I have developed over the years of the progression of God's giving commandments to man, beginning from the Garden of Eden. Man is given one commandment in the Garden of Eden: do not eat from the Tree of Knowledge of Good and Evil (Gen. 2:16-17; this is the simple reading; Rabbi Yochanan derives the Noahide laws from this verse, see *Sanhedrin* 56b). After the flood, Noah was given additional commandments: the permission to eat meat, the prohibition of eating flesh from a living creature, and the prohibition of murder (Gen. 9:3-6; see Maimonides *Hilkhot Melakhim*, chapter 9). The commandment to keep the calendar is given in Exodus 12, then some more commandments are given at Mara, followed by the full revelation at Sinai.

Perhaps this evolution of the imposition of a multiplicity of commandments reflects God's original expectations that mankind could extrapolate and figure out for himself what was expected of him. There is a rabbinic tradition that the forefathers fulfilled all of the commandments by their own deductions (see, e.g., Rashi on Gen. 26:5). Over time, as mankind grew spiritually more obtuse, the commandments had to be multiplied and spelled out. In effect, *Makkot* 23b-24a looks to reverse the ever-expanding process in order to ensure that the essence, the point, of Judaism not be lost due to the dramatic increase in numbers of commandments.

11. Hersh Goldwurm, *Schottenstein Edition of the Babylonian Talmud*, gen. ed. Nosson Scherman, Mesorah Publications, Brooklyn, NY, 1990, pp. 24a^1– 24a^5.

12. Robert Alter (*The Book of Psalms*, W.W. Norton, New York, 2007, p. 43, note on v. 2) writes on this Psalm, "The enumerated virtuous acts all pertain to a person's moral obligations to others." While the biblical text could be interpreted in this manner, the Talmud's examples have more to do with a person's relationship to God than with his fellow man.

13. Alan Morinis, in *Everyday Holiness: The Jewish Spiritual Path of Mussar* (Trumpeter, Boston, 2008, pp. 32-33) discusses how "visualizations" play an important role in how *musar* attempts to positively influence an individual:

> This ability to visualize is so important to *Mussar* practice that when R. Yechezkel Levenstein asks the question "What is the difference between a righteous person and a sinner?" he brings what he himself calls "a surprising answer" from the *Alter* of Kelm: "It is the ability to picture things in one's mind as if they were real."…

Perhaps this explains why in thirteen out of the twenty-four qualities mentioned in *Makkot* 23b-24a, different exemplars of these traits are mentioned. When one can visualize a story from the Bible or Chazal, it helps to concretize the behavior. (Of course, this begs the question why only some of the traits were presented in this manner and not all of them.)

14. "Does Jewish Tradition Recognize and Ethic Independent of Halacha?" in *Contemporary Jewish Ethics*, ed. Menachem Kellner, Sanhedrin Press, New York, 1978, pp. 102-23.

15. *The Morality of Law*, New Haven, 1964, pp. 5-9.

16. Kellner, p. 110.

17. See, e.g., Deut. 8:6; 19:9; 28:9.

18. http://www.nechama.org.il/cgi-bin/pagePrintMode.pl?Id=53

19. Exod. 23:4; Deut. 22:1-3.

20. See, e.g., *Sifrei* 45; Rashi on Deut. 22:2.

21. For Isaiah's list, only principle 13 is not accompanied by an historical example.

22. Three of the six lists are from the Minor Prophets: Micah, Amos, and Habakkuk. It is generally accepted that "minor" only means that their prophetic works are shorter than the other books of the prophets.

23. Although Abraham is the earliest biblical figure associated with humility, he is not the last. The Talmud contrasts the humility of Jewish leaders with the arrogance of non-Jewish leaders:

> The Holy One, blessed be He, said to Israel: I love you because even when I bestow greatness upon you, you humble yourselves before Me. I bestowed greatness upon Abraham, yet he said to Me, "I am but dust and ashes" (Gen. 18:27); on Moses and Aaron, yet they said, "And we are nothing" (Exod. 16:8); on David, yet he said, "But I am a worm and no man" (Psalm 22:7).
>
> But with the heathens it is not so. I bestowed greatness upon Nimrod, and he said, "Come, let us build us a city" (Gen. 11:4); on Pharaoh, and he said, "Who is the Lord?" (Exod. 5:2); on Sennacherib, and he said, "Who are they among all the gods of the countries?" (2 Kings 18:35); Upon Nebuchadnezzar, and he said, "I will ascend above the heights of the clouds" (Isa. 14:14); upon Hiram, king of Tyre, and he said, "I sit in the seat of God, in the heart of the seas" (*Chullin* 89a, quoting Ezek. 28:2)

The passage concludes by suggesting that at least two of Abraham's successors surpassed him when it came to humility:

> Rava, others say R. Yochanan, said: More significant is that which is said of Moses and Aaron than that which is said of Abraham. Of Abraham it is said, "I am but dust and ashes," whereas of Moses and Aaron it is said, "And we are nothing."

Whether or not Moses and Aaron were more humble than Abraham is beside the point. Abraham began an important moral tradition of humility that all Jews should emulate, which is the point of the verse in Micah.

24. See *Sanhedrin* 46b-47a.

25. See *Berakhot* 6b.

26. "The study of Torah may be suspended for escorting a dead body to the burying place and a bride to the canopy (*Megillah* 29a). The Meiri writes, "for escorting the bride from the home of her father to the home of her groom."

27. Hebrew, *mikhlal hein attah shome'a lav*. See, e.g., *Numbers Rabbah* 9:36.

28. There is a famous rabbinic teaching *she-lo lishmah ba lishmah*, even if a *mitzvah* is performed for the wrong reason, he will come to do it for the right reason (*Pesachim* 50b). However, the leaders of the *Musar* movement have questioned if this is always true. Regardless, it is clear that Habakkuk's verse posits the ideal situation to which we should all aspire.

29. See *Yalkut Shimoni*, 1 Samuel, #76.

Chapter 4

In All Your Ways Know Him

תלמוד בבלי מסכת ברכות דף סג עמוד א
דרש בר קפרא: איזוהי פרשה קטנה שכל גופי תורה תלוין בה –
(משלי ג, ו) "בכל דרכיך דעהו והוא יישר ארחותיך." אמר רבא:
אפילו לדבר עבירה.

עין יעקב שם[1]
אמר ר' פפא: היינו דאמרי אינשי גנבא אפום מחתרתא רחמנא קרי.

Babylonian Talmud, *Berakhot* 63a
Bar Kappara expounded: What short text is there upon which all the essential principles of the Torah depend? "In all your ways know Him and He will direct your paths" (Prov. 3:6). Rava remarked: Even for a matter of transgression.

***Ein Yaakov*'s Edition of the Talmud**
Said R. Pappa: This is what is meant when people say, "A thief just before he breaks in calls out to God."[2]

Moving from Abstract to Applied

The verses from Amos and Habakkuk focus upon man's need to understand God better on the one hand, and to develop a strong sense of faith in the Divine on the other. Both of these intensely spiritual qualities appear to be more general and attitudinal, rather than specific and practical. Similarly, based on Bar Kappara's statement in *Berakhot* 63a, one might think that "knowing God" is lacking specificity and deeply ambiguous. What does it mean to know God?

Bar Kappara & Man's Relationship with God

Before considering Proverbs 3:6 itself, it is appropriate to examine Bar Kappara's personality. What accounted for his emphasis on this verse as representing a central principle of Judaism? A significant dimension of Bar Kappara's personality emerges from his contribution to a discussion about the repetition of the *Amidah* (Silent Devotional Prayer). The rabbis of the Talmud are discussing the *Modim de-Rabbanan*.[3] The Talmud asks, "While the prayer leader recites *Modim anachnu Lach* [We give thanks to You] what does the congregation say?" (*Sotah* 40a). The Talmud then lists five different opinions, culminating in the comment of R. Pappa that the practice is to include all of the proposed prayers.[4] The Jerusalem Talmud records an additional set of four longer prayers for *Modim de-Rabbanan*, the longest by far being Bar Kappara's prayer:

> To You do we kneel; to You do we bend our bodies; to You do we prostrate ourselves; to You do we bend our knees. Because to You every knee bends, every tongue swears loyalty. To You is greatness and courage and eternity and

splendor. Because everything that is in the Heavens and the earth is Yours, and therefore the Kingship and the status of the One Who is exalted over all other leaders. Wealth and honor are Yours. You rule over all, and in Your hand is power and might, and it is within Your power to elevate and strengthen all. And now, our God, we give thanks to You and praise Your glorious Name. With our entire hearts and our entire souls we prostrate ourselves. "All my bones shall say: 'Lord, who is like unto You, Who delivers the poor from him that is too strong for him, the poor and the needy from him that takes his possessions?'" (Psalm 35:10). Blessed are You, God, the Lord to Whom we give thanks (Jerusalem Talmud, *Berakhot* 1:5).[5]

In addition to displaying his articulateness, the prayer suggests that Bar Kappara was deeply spiritual and extremely conscious of the role that God filled in his everyday life. Such a consciousness would very well draw his attention to Proverbs 3:6 as a central component of his religious experience.

Nevertheless, whatever the reason that Bar Kappara explicitly posited the centrality of Proverbs 3:6, we should try to understand the verse's meaning, and how it relates to the verses of Amos and Habakkuk in *Makkot*.

A Methodological Observation

Methodologically, when confronted with a difficult biblical phrase that is quoted in the Talmud or Midrash, we must see how the biblical commentators understood the verse, as well as the authoritative commentaries on the oral tradition. And if a commentator has written on both the Bible and Talmud, we are offered the additional dimension of comparing and contrasting how the same authority treated the verse in different circumstances.

Ibn Ezra (1089-1164)

As is often the case, Ibn Ezra does not waste words; but simultaneously, perhaps due to his terseness, he sometimes engages in allusion more than clear delineation. One must always be wary with respect to properly interpreting his extremely laconic statements. In this case, combining his interpretation of Proverbs 3:6 with what he writes on the following two verses (7-8) will shed the most light on his view. The full biblical passage is:

> (6) In all your ways know Him, and He will direct your paths. (7) Be not wise in your own eyes; fear the Lord, and depart from evil. (8) It shall be health to your navel, and marrow to your bones (Prov. 6:6-8).

Ibn Ezra writes:

> "In all your ways": In your activities and in your wisdom know Him [and] place Him on your scale [Heb., *al mishkal sa'eihu*].[6]
>
> "Be not wise in your own eyes": Lest you say, "Relying on my own wisdom will I direct my paths."
>
> "Depart from evil": from evil acts, and then God will cure you from all sickness.

For Ibn Ezra, "knowing God" means constantly asking oneself how God would react to what I am doing or thinking. It seems to me that this is an implication the verse, "And you shall do that which is right and good in the sight of the Lord" (Deut. 6:18), i.e., aside from carrying out the commandments in general, one should anticipate how God would desire one to think and act in situations where clear halakhic directives do not exist.[7] While human beings ultimately exercise autonomy and free will in their actions, God should not only figure as an afterthought when one evaluates how a particular action turned out.

Many observant individuals only engage in introspection regarding God's view of one's own actions when things have not worked out favorably. Following a disappointment, he wonders whether God and His Divine values should play a role for that individual's life in the future. Others, who claim to be scrupulous about *mitzvah*-observance, never consider incorporating God into their lives fully. They prefer to compartmentalize, allowing religious considerations to impact their lives on a limited basis, if at all. Ibn Ezra would obviously object to a life that is either compartmentalized or unreflective. He articulates the expectation that God influence all decisions and commitments that an individual undertakes.

Ibn Ezra's conception of knowing God is reminiscent of a talmudic comment regarding the best way one should live his life:

> Our Rabbis taught: For two and a half years were Bet Shammai and Bet Hillel in dispute, the former asserting that it was better for man not to have been created than to have been created, and the latter maintaining that it is better for man to have been created than not to have been created. They finally took a vote and decided that it was better for man not to have been created than to have been created, but now that he has been created, let him

investigate his past deeds or, as others say, let him examine his future actions (*Eruvin* 13b).

Could this have been what Bar Kappara felt was so fundamental about Proverbs 3:6? The commandments of Judaism are not ends in themselves, but means by which an individual can constantly remind himself of God's presence and thereby introduce God into all that he does before he does it.[8]

Since Plato was a student of Socrates, it is possible that he heard directly from his teacher, "the greatest good of a man is daily to converse about virtue, and all that concerning which you hear me examining myself and others, and that the life which is unexamined is not worth living…" (*Apology* 37e-38a).

Ibn Ezra views the parallel sentiment in Proverbs as not simply requiring man to be philosophically reflective about his life, but to apply Godly criteria to his activities in order to act and think in ways that will make himself as well as the world holier and closer to God.

How does Ibn Ezra's interpretation reconcile with Rava's comment, that someone knows God "even for a matter of transgression"? If this person "knows God" in accordance with Ibn Ezra's formulation, he would dissuade himself from sin. More difficult is R. Pappa's statement recorded in *Ein Yaakov* that before the transgressor actually carries out his sin, he prays to God to be successful. Rather than God serving as a touchstone for right and wrong, such a practice appears to constitute the ultimate form of compartmentalization, whereby the sinner literally prays for success, without regard for the morality of the act itself.[9]

Rabbenu Yonah (d. 1263)

In Rabbenu Yonah's commentary on Proverbs 3:6, he advances three separate interpretations for the phrase "in all your ways know Him," supplying us with three distinct understandings of Bar Kappara's comment in *Berakhot* 63a.[10]

Rabbenu Yonah's First Interpretation

Rabbenu Yonah's first interpretation of Proverbs 3:6 reads:

> In every action that you wish to do, remember God, who is blessed, and depend upon Him that He will cause you to be successful in this endeavor, place upon Him your trust, and cause your heart to return to him, because that action [that you do] is not really up to you. This verse adds to what the text had stated earlier, "Trust in the Lord with all your heart, and lean not upon your own understanding" (Prov. 3:5). For there are some who generally trust in God, and believe that all is in God's hands and trust in Him, and they don't trust in men and not in their own strength or understanding; yet they do not manifest such trust in their hearts regarding the details, specific situations, i.e., in every action that they undertake....
>
> And know that there are people who look towards God regarding matters on a grand scale. For example, [when] they intend to take a sea voyage to seek merchandise or to journey with a caravan, yet with respect to smaller things, they do not remember God, because the matter is insignificant in their eyes, and it is clear in their minds that these small enterprises will succeed, or because they are not risking a great loss should this smaller matter not take place or not prove successful....

In this first interpretation, Rabbenu Yonah posits that "knowing God" means "trusting in God." In his view, Proverbs 3:5-6 is criticizing people who claim to trust in God, even though they give no evidence of such trust in their personal behavior. Or, alternately, they might trust in God for very large undertakings, but not when it comes to lesser matters. The Chazon Ish (Rabbi Avraham Yeshaya Karelitz, 1878-1953) provides a practical illustration of one aspect of what Rabbenu Yonah is discussing:

> And regarding what we see in real life, Reuven, a man professing values of *musar*, and who constantly speaks about trust [*bitachon*] in God, criticizes the self-reliant efforts undertaken by many, and claims to be repulsed by their pursuit of money. He is successful, his store not lacking for merchandise and he generally does not have to exert himself in his business pursuits. He loves the idea of trust in God, since it has shone upon him with favor.
>
> And behold, we are suddenly surprised to see trustful Reuven plotting with his young men and advisors to confound the plans of his colleague, who wishes to open a store like Reuven's, and this upsets him. Initially these feelings are only in his heart because he is embarrassed to allow others to discern these feelings, lest he will be humiliated in the eyes of those who know him; but in the end he even loses his sense of embarrassment, and he begins to engage in overt deliberate efforts to stop his competition. And little by little he becomes ever more open, and embarrassment vanishes from his heart, and he overtly engages in disagreeable actions and lowly strategies

for all to see. The competition between him and his colleague becomes very public and is the subject of much conversation, without any end in sight, and he fabricates false reasons and inferences to justify his actions.[11]

Perhaps Bar Kappara, according to Rabbenu Yonah's first interpretation, would maintain, as Chazon Ish illustrates, that one is not only to pay lip service to knowing God and His ways, but he has to also actually lead his life according to those principles. Furthermore, *bitachon* must be pursued at all times, not only when it is easy to achieve, but even when it entails sacrifice, personal risk, and loss. Trust in God remains a religious value, even when everything one has become accustomed to is being threatened.

The Chazon Ish's example of Reuven segues directly to the situation presented by Rava in *Berakhot* 63a. A thief decides to take what is not his because he is not prepared to accept the legal constraints of his situation.[12]

If one were to be industrious rather than plot against his competitor, he too would likely be successful, and would not look to steal the property of others. The criminal, however, has convinced himself that success is impossible without theft, or that honest labor would take too long to fulfill his desires, and therefore he pursues immediate gratification by breaking the law. The issue of *bitachon* does not enter into his calculations at all; he has chosen illegal efforts instead of trusting in God that his desires will eventually be satisfied (and even if they aren't, that he still must not covet his neighbor's property).

R. Yonah's Second Interpretation (and its Two Dimensions)

Rabbenu Yonah continues:

> Another way to interpret "in all your ways know Him" is to derive from it that all of your actions should be for the sake of Heaven. Do not seek this-worldly pleasure, enjoyment, honor, wealth, or any possession, other than to engage in service of God, may He be blessed, "and He will guide your paths," i.e., aside from the great reward one receives for thinking in this manner, your enterprise will succeed when you carry it out for the sake of Heaven.

Rabbenu Yonah turns from a consideration of *bitachon* to discuss what a person chooses to do with his life, with the opportunities and abilities he has been given. "Knowing God" becomes a term for devoting oneself, one's talents and abilities to God.

In effect, this second interpretation gives broader meaning to how the Torah describes man's choices. In Deuteronomy, God states that man has two paths before him:

> See, I [Moses] have set before you this day life and good, and death and evil, in that I command you this day: [1] to love the Lord your God, [2] to walk in His ways, and [3] to keep His commandments and His statutes and His ordinances; then you shall live and multiply, and the Lord your God shall bless you in the land wherever you go in to possess it. But if your heart turn away, and you will not hear, but shall be drawn away, and worship other gods, and serve them, I declare unto you this day, that you shall

surely perish; you shall not prolong your days upon the land, wherever you pass over the Jordan to go in to possess it. I call heaven and earth to witness against you this day, that I have set before you life and death, the blessing and the curse; therefore choose life, that you may live, you and your seed, [1] to love the Lord your God, [3'] to hearken to His voice, and [2'] to cleave unto Him; for that is your life, and the length of your days; that you may dwell in the land which the Lord swore unto your fathers, to Abraham, to Isaac, and to Jacob, to give them (Deut. 30:15-20).

Rabbenu Yonah points out that the Torah not only conveys the abstract dialectical pairings of "life and death" and "blessing and curse," but also defines them in clearer and more specific terms.[13] The general terms "life" and "blessing" are refined by three actions: loving God, walking in His ways (or "cleaving to Him"), and keeping His commandments (or "hearkening to his voice").

The third category, following God's commandments, does not leave much to the imagination. However, the first two actions are more difficult to understand. What does it mean to love God and walk in His ways? A strong argument could be made, based on *Sotah* 14a, that walking in God's ways parallels Rabbenu Yonah's second interpretation of Proverbs 3:6. From Deuteronomy 30, it can be demonstrated that "choosing life" entails more than complying with the Torah's commandments. The most appropriate way to "walk in God's ways" may be to incorporate thoughts about God into all of one's actions.

The *Baal ha-Turim* (Rabbi Jacob ben Asher, c. 1269-c. 1343) was so moved by Rabbenu Yonah's interpretation that he actually codified a variant of it in his work on Jewish law, called the *Tur*[14]:

> In all aspects of deriving pleasure from worldly pursuits, one should not intend to gain pleasure for himself, but for the sake of serving the exalted Creator, as is written, "In all thy ways know Him…" (Prov. 3:6). And the Rabbis, may their memory be a blessing, said, "And all of your actions should be for the sake of Heaven" (*Avot* 2:12). And so explained Rabbenu Yonah in his commentary on *Avot*: "And all of your actions should be for the sake of Heaven" — Even matters that are optional [in contrast to obligations], such as eating, drinking, walking, sitting, standing, marital intimacy, conversation and all of the requirements of your body, they should all be to further serving your Creator, or at least something that will cause His service. How does this apply to eating and drinking? It goes without saying that one should not eat or drink substances that are prohibited, but even when one eats and drinks foods that are permitted, and one is hungry and thirsty, if he consumes these things simply to obtain pleasure for his body, this is not praiseworthy, unless he intends to fulfill the needs of his body and eats in order that he should continue to live all for the purpose of serving his Creator (*Tur, Orach Chaim* 231).[15]

The *Tur* interprets the verse as the basis for Bar Kappara's dictum that the religious ideal it not to compartmentalize or dichotomize one's life into holy and profane segments,[16] but to sanctify every aspect of life. According to this reading, one should constantly and proactively find opportunities to serve God, if not overtly by fulfilling a particular commandment, then indirectly by identifying the motivation for doing an optional action as yet another form of serving God. Furthermore, in light of the *Tur*'s presentation, Rabbenu Yonah's explanation is not an innovation, but was already anticipated in *Avot* 2:12 by R. Yosi.

The *Tur*, in understanding Proverbs 3:6, appears to take the *Pnei Moshe*'s view of Ben Azzai, but one step further. We had surmised that according to the *Pnei Moshe*, every interaction with another human being becomes an opportunity to think about and deepen our appreciation of God. The *Tur* widens this mindset to include everything that one does, whether he is relating to other human beings, or even when he is alone, devoid of human companionship. Because man has the mental capacities of abstract thought and imagination,[17] if he turns his thoughts to God, whether he is engaged in obligatory or optional actions, he is *mekaddesh* the *chol* (sanctifying the non-holy),[18] and transforms all that he does into *avodat Hashem* (serving God). By constantly calling God to mind, one comes to very frequently remember what God represents and does, and in turn will emulate His ways throughout life.

However, the *Tur*'s approach is not helpful addressing Rava's addendum, that someone should know His ways, "even for a matter of transgression." While there is a rabbinic concept of *aveirah lishmah* (a sin for the sake of Heaven),[19] such examples are rare. Bar Kappara's interpretation of Proverbs, by contrast, addresses instances of permitted rather than forbidden behavior. This assumption is further clarified by the alternate text in *Ein Yaakov*, observing that even the thief prays for Divine assistance before embarking upon his sinful endeavor.[20] Such a statement hopefully describes an aberration rather than a norm.

The *baalei musar* (authors of works directed at improving personal character traits and religious practice) were very judgmental when it came to people treating one another dishonestly, since such actions had become ubiquitous. For example, Rabbi Moshe Chaim Luzzatto wrote:

> Although we see that most people are not manifest thieves in the sense of openly confiscating their neighbors' belongings and depositing them among their own possessions, *most of them* get the taste of theft in the course of their business dealings by allowing themselves to gain through their neighbors' loss, saying, "Business is different...."[21]

This is another example of compartmentalization. Therefore, while Rabbenu Yonah's second understanding is the springboard for the *Tur*, his interpretation of *Berakhot* 63a does not seem to have had an influence on people's behavior.

R. Yonah's Second Interpretation (and its Second Dimension)

Rabbenu Yonah continues, in his second interpretation:

> It is also appropriate to explain "in all your ways know Him": do not forget due to your preoccupation with your work, the remembrance of the yoke of Heaven, fear of Him and His exaltedness. Only then "He will guide your paths" and thereby your work will meet with success, as the Rabbis said, "Our Rabbis taught: The pious men of old used to wait for an hour and pray for an hour and then wait again for an hour" (*Berakhot* 32b). But seeing that they spend nine hours a day[22] over prayer, how is their

knowledge of Torah preserved and how is their work done? Because they are pious, their Torah is preserved and their work is blessed.[23]

In this case, "knowing God" becomes an expectation to be "conscious of God" throughout the course of an activity or project. Whereas the first part of Rabbenu Yonah's second explanation deals with what a person should be thinking when he begins to undertake some sort of task or behavior, the second part focuses on what a person should be thinking during his involvement in that project. Understandably, if the task is complex or long-lasting, it would be normal for him to be focused on the task rather than meditating on God during the entire project. It is probably more difficult to fulfill this part of Rabbenu Yonah's explanation than to inject spirituality at the outset of some project or behavior.

One could posit that many *mitzvot* throughout the day serve as reminders to bring God into one's life: studying Torah, making blessings, and praying (especially *Minchah*, which requires one to interrupt his work day), and wearing a *kippah* and *tzitzit* (for men) are some examples. These rituals inject spirituality and consciousness of God, so the individual will continue to think about God even during the busiest periods of the day.

Based on this comment of Rabbenu Yonah, Rava's addition, that even a thief prays, would not appear to be possible. How can one think of God throughout the performance of a transgression? While one might feel guilty after the fact, thoughts of God either before or during should bring a quick halt to the sinful activity, rather than allowing the individual to see it through.

The Great Principle of the Torah

Rabbenu Yonah's Third Interpretation

Rabbenu Yonah's final interpretation is:

> It is possible to interpret "in all thy ways know Him": at the beginning of each action, take to heart whether there is some iniquity that one is transgressing by performing this action, and do not undertake it until it is clear to you that it is desirable before God. Only then will it succeed and "He will guide your paths."

This time, "knowing God" means referencing God's Law before any undertaking. It appears to me that this interpretation of Proverbs 3:6 is the narrowest and least evocative of the three offered by this commentator. As the passage from Rabbenu Yonah's commentary on *Avot*, quoted by the *Tur* above, states, "It goes without saying that one should not eat or drink substances that are prohibited...."

If the author of Proverbs wishes to advise the reader of something he might not have known, how is it innovative to remind him to observe Jewish law? And if the intention is to remind the individual to reflect on what he is about to do, rather than simply plunge ahead and thereby unthinkingly commit transgressions,[24] this again appears to me to be obvious.

I would like to suggest an understanding of Rabbenu Yonah's final interpretation, in light of the surrounding verses, that would add an extra dimension to our analysis of what Ibn Ezra wrote as well:

> Trust in the Lord with all your heart, and lean not upon your own understanding. In all your ways know Him, and He will direct your paths. Be not wise in your own eyes; fear the Lord, and depart from evil (Prov. 3:5-7).

Let us assume that the individual is God-fearing and wishes to comply with Torah law at all times. However, he prefers to rely on his own understanding and wisdom to determine whether or not something is permitted or prohibited, rather than consulting with another party. Even if he happens to be a great scholar, Jewish tradition assumes that each of us is subjective when it comes to our own affairs, as Rava said, *adam karov etzel atzmo*, "an individual is considered a relative to himself" (*Sanhedrin* 9b).[25] In addition to a lack of objectivity, there are the very natural human qualities of rationalization and self-justification when someone draws a favorable conclusion for himself, as reflected in the talmudic dictum, *ein adam meisim atzmo rasha*, "No person can/will declare himself evil."[26]

For these reasons, the Mishnah advises us, "Joshua b. Perahia says: Establish for yourself a teacher, and acquire a friend, and judge every person favorably" (*Avot* 1:6). A subsequent Mishnah repeats, "R. Gamliel says: Establish for yourself a teacher and thereby remove yourself from doubt..." (*Avot* 1:16).

Rabbi Baruch ha-Levi Epstein (1860-1941, most noted as the author of the *Torah Temimah*), wrote in his commentary on *Avot* (called *Baruch she-Amar*):

> And according to what was explained regarding the understanding of the expression "Establish for yourself a teacher," it will equally serve to explain the nearby Mishnah, "Establish for yourself a teacher and thereby remove yourself from doubt"... because when you establish for yourself a permanent teacher, to listen to him and to accept his views, he will resolve for you your doubts in Torah and in life, and you will thereby be removed from

doubt, because he will "direct your paths" as is written, "In all your ways know Him and He will direct your paths" (Prov. 3:6), and the opinion of your teacher is comparable to the opinion of Heaven, as it is written, "Whomever argues with his teacher is comparable to arguing with Heaven; and whomever suspects his teacher is comparable to suspecting Heaven" (*Sanhedrin* 101a).[27]

In other words, even if one wishes to follow God's directions in terms of the choices that he is confronted with, in an age of *hester panim* (God's hiding His face),[28] how can that direction be objectively determined? If the situation is a matter of definitive law, then a scholarly individual with access to a library would be able to readily look up how to proceed in the situation in which he finds himself and act accordingly. But as Nachmanides, in a source cited in full earlier, astutely points out, the Torah did not address all possible situations that could arise in someone's life (on Deut. 6:18).

A great deal of halakhic decisions will require someone to apply written statutes to real-life situations. Relying on an expert halakhic guide with personal integrity becomes the only way that one can have confidence that God will direct his paths. Perhaps Ibn Ezra and Rabbenu Yonah (third opinion) are advancing that one should include an objective halakhic authority when one is thinking about how to proceed in a certain matter.

Talmudic Commentaries

Since Bar Kappara cites a single verse as the basis for "all the essential principles of the Torah," it is methodologically valid to consider how classic biblical commentators approached the verse.

This can illuminate the proper meaning of the biblical verse in context. However, one must also consider the talmudic passage where the verse appears, especially because some rabbinic passages take liberties with the simple meaning of the verse. In addition, the talmudic commentaries will take into account not just Bar Kappara, but also Rava and R. Pappa.

Rashi on *Berakhot* 63a[29]

In his commentary on the Talmud, Rashi writes:

> Pay attention to whether this is necessary for a *mitzvah*, like Elijah on Mt. Carmel, [and if you conclude that it is necessary] then transgress it (!).

Strikingly, Rashi raises the issue of *hora'at sha'ah*.[30] He is referring to Elijah's confrontation of the false prophets of Baal (see 1 Kings 18). Elijah challenged the prophets of Baal, but he offered sacrifices outside of the Temple, which is normally forbidden (Deut. 12:13-14). Since this prohibition was temporarily suspended for Elijah, his actions are known as a *hora'at sha'ah*, either because Elijah set aside the law for a greater good, or because God allowed His law to be suspended to defeat the prophets of Baal.

How Broad is *Hora'at Sha'ah*?

Rashi applies Prov. 3:6 to the case of Elijah on Mt. Carmel. Based on this reading, Elijah had to ask himself, based on his own knowledge of God, if his actions were proper in this case. It would appear that Rashi is presenting a variation on Ibn Ezra and Rabbenu Yonah (third interpretation). In other words, Elijah didn't use his knowledge of God to dissuade himself from doing something prohibited, but instead to authorize its performance.

But serious questions arise from this. Certainly Elijah was a distinguished Jewish prophet who had experienced Divine Revelation, so he knew when a *hora'at sha'ah* could be applied. But Rashi is commenting on the Talmud's quotation of Proverbs, a book directed not at prophets, but at the common man. He seems to suggest that not only prophets, but ordinary individuals as well, are empowered by Prov. 3:6 to make the calculation whether God would approve of a temporary suspension of a commandment; if the individual thinks that God approves, then the individual has license to transgress it. Wouldn't the situation have to be extreme, comparable to attempting to refute idolatrous sympathies and practices of the Jewish people, as was the case with Elijah? Furthermore, wouldn't the individual need to possess a great degree of gravitas and personal assuredness, like Elijah, before allowing himself to enact such an approach?

Maimonides is prepared to empower only a *bet din* (Jewish court) with the ability to declare a *hora'at sha'ah*:

> A court may, however, suspend the application of such [rabbinic] decrees [legislated by previous courts] temporarily, even if it [the current court] is of lesser stature than the original court. The rationale is that these decrees should not be considered as more severe than the words of the Torah itself, and any court has the authority to abrogate the words of the Torah as a temporary measure.
>
> What is implied? If a court sees that it is necessary to strengthen the faith and create a safeguard so that the people will not violate Torah law, they may apply beatings

and punishments that are not sanctioned by Torah. They may not, however, establish the matter for posterity and say that this is the *halakhah*.

Similarly, if they saw that temporarily it was necessary to nullify a positive commandment or violate a negative commandment in order to bring people at large back to the Jewish faith or to prevent many Jews from transgressing in other matters, they may do what is necessary at that time. To explain by analogy: Just like a doctor may amputate a person's hand or foot so that the person as a whole will live; so, too, at times, the court may rule to temporarily violate some of the commandments so that they will later keep all of them. In this vein, the Sages of the previous generations said, "Desecrate one Sabbath for a person's sake so that he will keep many Sabbaths"[31] (*Mamrim* 2:4).

Although under certain circumstances, a single judge can adjudicate a case,[32] usually a court must consist of at least three judges, and the deliberations will more assure a responsible decision as to whether to issue a *hora'at sha'ah*. For Rashi to suggest that a single person, who is neither prophet nor judge, can determine for himself whether or not God would approve such a decision, is difficult to imagine.

Furthermore, would Rashi's interpretation apply to Rava's comment that even a thief should proceed, after he had concluded God will approve of his crime?[33] There are clearly some cases where someone is permitted to violate a biblical law, like if a sick person must eat on Yom Kippur. But could the same be said about someone who is a professional thief? Furthermore, it seems that Rashi would be even more hard-pressed to account for *Ein Yaakov*'s addition that a thief prays for God's blessing before committing a crime. This addition does not provide a further case where *hora'at sha'ah* is permitted, but illustrates how ludicrous it is for an individual to invoke God in such unacceptable circumstances.

Tzlach on *Berakhot* 63a

Rabbi Yechezkel Segal Landau (1718-1793, known as the *Noda bi-Yehudah* after his collection of responsa) in his commentary on the Talmud called *Tziyyun le-Nefesh Chayah* (abbreviated *Tzlach*) has a different interpretation of this passage:

> And there are those who apply this even to a transgression, that is to say, even when one is engaged in committing a transgression, he should recall this thing, i.e., his strength and his life at that moment comes to him through Divine supervision and intention of the Blessed One. And this should serve his interests—perhaps he will be embarrassed and humiliated from before his Creator, may He be blessed, and he will desist. And even if his passion overcomes him and he does not change his mind, this belief and memory will stand him in good stead so that he will immediately regret afterwards what he has done….

Whereas Rashi focuses on Bar Kappara's statement itself, allowing for a robust comparison with the biblical commentaries of Ibn Ezra and Rabbenu Yonah, the *Tzlach* specifically addresses Rava. (Only talmudic commentators would comment on Rava, since the biblical interpreters were not directly confronted by either Rava or R. Pappa.)

In all Your Ways Know Him

The *Tzlach* takes the approach ostensibly offered by Rabbenu Yonah's first interpretation, but focuses on Rava's words, applying it to a thief or someone considering sin. Earlier we wondered how *bitachon* applies to an individual who failed to internalize a religious attitude, and instead took matters into his own hands by way of sin. The *Tzlach* assumes that the potential thief will abandon his criminal plans, once he acknowledges that his existence is due to God. And even if he follows through on his intentions, at least he will feel extremely guilty after the fact, and be ready to repent.

When we combine Rabbenu Yonah and the *Tzlach* in their interpretations of Bar Kappara and Rava, it emerges that there are three levels of *bitachon*, or how one understands "He will direct your paths":

a) Ideal: A person's trust in God is so powerful and clear that he completely relies on the Divine for the choices he makes and everything that he does;

b) Average: While *bitachon* does not comprise an individual's primary motivation, in the end it serves as a corrective and prevents the person from violating halakhic norms;

c) Minimal: *Bitachon* is not strong enough to stop him from transgressing, but it serves as the basis of guilt after the fact, which ultimately leads to repentance.

As for the folk-saying in *Ein Yaakov*, obviously (a) and (b) will not apply, but perhaps (c) is relevant, in the sense that for some thieves, there is ambivalence about what they do, and perhaps even an unspoken desire to be saved from wickedness.

The Great Principle of the Torah

Iyun Yaakov on *Berakhot* 63a

Rabbi Jacob b. Joseph Reischer (d. 1733), wrote a commentary on the *Ein Yaakov*, called the *Iyun Yaakov*. In it he writes the following on our passage:

> This means that he should take to heart that everything that occurs in this world, all is done and succeeds by the Divine supervision of the Holy One, blessed be He, and without Him nothing can take place. Assuming this, if he wishes to commit a crime like stealthily stealing or holding someone up in the open, he should know that if this is not God's will, then he will not succeed. This realization will cause him to repent from sin, because from Him, evil will not result, and through such thinking, "He will direct your ways" to repent.

The *Iyun Yaakov*, like the *Tzlach*, also concentrates on Rava's case. He too develops the first interpretation of Rabbenu Yonah, specifically under what circumstances an individual should expect that his actions will succeed. Why would a person undertake an action if he believes that he will fail? While desperate men may proceed even when the odds of success are terribly slim, the more even-tempered individual would think twice.

Yet it seems that the *Tzlach* and *Iyun Yaakov* raise the problem of theodicy (why bad things happen to good people). Rabbenu Yonah's representation of *bitachon*, echoed by the *Tzlach* and *Iyun Yaakov*, is fundamental to the religious outlook. However, it is hard to find empirical evidence to prove that people who follow God's law succeed, while those who sin will fail. And even if it were contended that in the long run, *bitachon* would be rewarded, would this suffice for a short-term thinker, like a thief? Someone who is prepared to steal possesses a low level of *bitachon*. Will the consideration that God always causes the sinner to fail actually dissuade him before the fact or even inspire repentance afterwards?

Implications for Contemporary Jews

Bar Kappara in *Berakhot* 63a challenges us to think about ourselves in such a way where God can serve as a guide to not only our ritual lives, but also our everyday actions. Almost everything that we do during our waking hours has halakhic and spiritual implications and therefore deserves reflection before, during, and after we do it. While that reflection can be conducted privately, there is value for us to concretize it by consulting with someone trained in Jewish law and values, and whom we respect and feel that he understands our personalities.

A second implication is that *bitachon* is extremely central to Jewish living and thought. This idea clashes culturally with the emphasis in our society on autonomy and self-reliance. In that sense, traditional Judaism must be viewed, at least to some degree, as seriously counter-cultural, demanding us to acknowledge that God, His laws, and His values, must play a dominant role in the way that we live our lives.

An additional challenge is to incorporate a strong sense of *bitachon* into our lives, despite the dialectics of success and failure, and that reward and punishment do not always appear to align with observed reality. A significant leap of faith is required, and perhaps strategies for how to encourage such faith should be developed.

Fourth, *bitachon* is not only something to be articulated, but also to be believed in and lived. Hypocrisy in this matter is probably common and predictable; however, it is a religious value that must be concretized in real life as much as possible, particularly when it requires us to act against our short-term best interests.

A fifth conclusion is that, if we are unable to comply with the demands of Jewish law, we ought to honestly evaluate where we stand religiously and ethically, and strategize for improvement in the future. A sense of *bitachon* can keep us connected to God, however tenuously. Even if a halakhic lifestyle is not currently desirable for an individual, nevertheless belief and commitment fluctuate throughout our lives, and it would be imprudent for him to discard everything just because he currently has different priorities. According to Rava, and especially the view recorded in *Ein Yaakov*, hope for future spiritual refinement is entirely possible, even when it seems to be improbable.

Endnotes

1. *Ein Yaakov* is an aggadic collection by Rabbi Jacob ibn Habib (c. 1460-1516). In this passage, the *Ein Yaakov* has a phrase that is not in the standard Vilna edition. This passage in included in parentheses, meaning it might not be authentic. Nevertheless R. Pappa's comment adds a worthwhile dimension to the discussion.

2. This comment is reminiscent of the Bob Dylan song, "With God on Our Side" (1964) which contains the line, "For you don't count the dead / When God's on your side."

3. The *Amidah* is first recited quietly and then repeated in public by the prayer leader. However, the *Modim* (Thanksgiving) section is different, since at that point, the individuals recite a *Modim* that differs from the public recitation. According to the Avudraham, this is because when it comes to giving thanks to God, that cannot be done through an emissary, but each Jew must do that individually.

4. The five proposals are as follows:

The Talmud's Suggestions	Contemporary Ashkenazi Liturgy
1. Rav declared: "We give thanks to You, O Lord our God, because we are able to give You thanks	We give thanks to You for You are the Lord, our God and God of our fathers,
2. Samuel declared: "God of all flesh, seeing that we give You thanks."	God of all flesh,
3. R. Simlai declared: "Our Creator and Creator of all things in the beginning, seeing that we give You thanks."	who formed us and formed the universe.

4. The men of Nehardea declared in the name of R. Simlai, "Blessings and thanksgivings to Your Great Name because You have kept us alive and preserved us, seeing that we give You thanks."	Blessings and thanks are due to Your great and holy Name for giving us life and sustaining us.
5. R. Acha b. Yaakov used to conclude thus: "So may You continue to keep us alive and be gracious to us, and gather us together and assemble our exiles to Your holy courts to observe Your statutes and to do your will with a perfect heart, seeing that we give You thanks."	May You continue to give us life and sustain us; and may You gather our exiles to Your holy courts, to keep your statutes, to do Your will and serve You with a perfect heart, for it is for us to give You thanks. Blessed is God to whom thanksgiving is due.

5, Bar Kappara had the reputation of being a magnificent wordsmith. See *Leviticus Rabbah* 28:2.

6. In other words, would God approve of the actions one is about to take.

7. See Nachmanides' second interpretation on this verse, cited in Chapter 1.

8. In Chapter 2, we quoted Nachmanides to the effect that the purpose of the commandments was to "believe in our God and affirm to Him that He is our Creator." Looking at this statement through the lens of Ibn Ezra, we are not only expected to believe in God, but also apply that belief to our actions to make sure that they are holy and Godly.

9. It has already been noted that R. Pappa's statement is apocryphal, and might not be a real problem, if he never actually said such a thing.

10. Rabbenu Yonah himself cites Bar Kappara within the context of his first interpretation and refers to him again in his summarizing statement at the end of his commentary for this verse, "Certainly, the

first interpretation that we wrote is contextually correct with respect to the rest of the chapter in Proverbs and follows the way of our Sages.... " He is arguing that *bitachon* is certainly a central tenet of Jewish belief and practice.

11. *Sefer Chazon Ish al Inyanei Emunah, Bitachon ve-Od*, Chapter 2, Section 3, ed. R. Sh. Grinman, Tel Aviv, 5739, p. 18.

12. This is what Ben Zoma intends when he states in *Avot* 4:1, "Who is wealthy? He who is satisfied with his portion, as it is said, 'When you eat the labor of your hands, happy shall you be, and it shall be well with you'" (Psalm 128:2).

13. This is essentially a *kelal u-frat*, starting with the general and moving on to the specific. This hermeneutic is generally applied to legal reasoning, but can by way of analogy be applied here as well.

14. The *Tur* quotes from Rabbenu Yonah's commentary on *Avot*, not Proverbs, but the essence is the same.

15. This *siman* in the *Tur* follows discussions of getting up in the morning, which includes *tzitzit, tefillin, Shacharit, kriyat ha-Torah, birkat kohanim*, laws of the synagogue, ritual hand-washing, and eating a meal. It is assumed that one's morning activities are standardized through breakfast. At that point, when most actions are optional rather than obligatory, it becomes important to consider the verse, "in all your ways know Him."

16. See my article "Integration of Judaic and General Studies in the Modern Orthodox Day School," in *Jewish Education*, Vol. 54, No. 4, Winter 1986, pp. 15-26, available at the time of publication of this book at http://www.lookstein.org/integration/bieler.htm

17. According to some, this is the meaning of being created in the "image of God" at the end of the verse cited by Ben Azzai (Gen. 5:1).

18. I have often used as an example a particular behavior that is codified in the *Shulchan Aruch*, and has been derided by many as overly compulsive, as exemplifying just this point: "One should put on his right shoe first without tying it. Afterwards he should put on his left shoe and tie it, and only then go on to tie the right shoe" (*Shulchan Aruch, Orach Chaim* 2:4).

The *Mishnah Berurah* writes:

> For so we find in the Torah that the right side is always given precedence regarding the thumb of the hand and the foot [e.g., Lev. 8:23-4], and in all other matters where the right side is preferred over the left [e.g. Deut. 25:9, *Yevamot* 104a]..... When it comes to tying, we find that the Torah gives precedence to the left side, for that is where one affixes the *tefillin* for the hand [if the person is right-handed] (*Mishnah Berurah, ad loc*, 5-6).

Again, a relatively trivial action, i.e., deciding which way to turn when there is no particular reason to choose one side over the other, by association with significant Jewish ritual, becomes deeply symbolic, reminding an individual of what took place in the Temple so long ago, a *zekher le-Mikdash* (a commemoration of the Temple).

19. In a curious passage, the Talmud records:

> R. Nachman b. Yitzchak said: A transgression performed with good intention [*lishmah*] is better than a precept performed with evil intention. But has not Rav Yehudah, citing Rav, said: A man should always occupy himself with the Torah and [its] precepts, even though it be for an ulterior motive [*lo lishmah*], for the result will be that he will eventually do them without ulterior motive? Read then: [A transgression performed with good intention is] as good as a precept performed for an ulterior motive, as it is written, "Blessed above women shall Yael be, the wife of Chever the Kenite. Above women in the tent shall she

be blessed" (Judges 5:24), and by "women in the tent," Sarah, Rebekah, Rachel, and Leah are meant (*Nazir* 23b).

20. Praying for the success of an illegal, immoral endeavor is a classic instance of someone who has missed the point. Consider a talmudic parallel:

> R. Eliezer says: If one stole a *se'ah* [a measure] of wheat, ground and baked it and set apart the *challah* [priestly gift], what benediction can he pronounce? This man would not be blessing, but blaspheming, and of him it is written, "The robber [*botze'a*] who blesses, condemns the Lord" (*Sanhedrin* 6b, quoting Psalm 10:30).

In both instances, the individual should not engage in thievery in the first place, rather than be concerned about pronouncing a blessing or receiving Divine assistance.

21. Available as of the publication of this book at http://www.shechem.org/torah/mesyesh/11.htm

22. Three hours each for the three standard prayers of *Shacharit, Minchah* and *Ma'ariv*.

23. This appears to side with the position of R. Shimon bar Yochai stated later in the same tractate:

> Our Rabbis taught: "And you shall gather in your corn" (Deut. 11:14). What is to be learned from these words? Since it says, "This book of the law shall not depart out from your mouth" (Josh. 1:8), I might think that this injunction is to be taken literally. Therefore it says, "And you shall gather in your corn," which implies that you are to combine the study of them with a worldly occupation. This is the view of R. Ishmael. R. Shimon b.

Yochai says: Is that possible? If a man ploughs in the ploughing season, and sows in the sowing season, and reaps in the reaping season, and threshes in the threshing season, and winnows in the season of wind, what is to become of the Torah? No; but when Israel performs the will of the Omnipresent, their work is performed by others, as it says, "And strangers shall stand and feed your flocks..." (Isa. 61:5), and when Israel does not perform the will of the Omnipresent their work is carried out by themselves, as it says, "And you shall gather in your corn." Nor is this all, but the work of others also is done by them, as it says, "And you shall serve your enemy..." (Deut. 28:48).

Said Abaye: Many have followed the advice of R. Ishmael, and it has worked well; others have followed R. Shimon b. Yochai and it has not been successful.

Rava said to the Rabbis: I would ask you not to appear before me during *Nisan* and *Tishrei* so that you may not be anxious about your food supply during the rest of the year (*Berakhot* 35b).

From the comments of Abaye and Rava, it would appear that R. Shimon b. Yochai's view did not become normative.

24. Such an idea echoes an implication in Ibn Ezra's more general interpretation discussed earlier. See also *Eruvin* 13b, quoted above.

25. Rava's statement in context means that a person is disqualified from testifying about himself, since he is biased. The underlying psychological rationale is that a person is biased in assessing his own actions.

26. Like the statement above, this means that a person legally cannot incriminate himself, and if he does, his testimony is invalid. However, it is appropriate to apply the legal principle to psychological situations outside the courtroom as well.

27. *Baruch she-Amar: Pirkei Avot*, Am Olam, Tel Aviv, pp. 31-2.

28. The state of the relationship between God and Israel is described as follows: "Then My anger shall be kindled against them in that day, and I will forsake them, and I will hide My face from them, and they shall be devoured, and many evils and troubles shall come upon them; so that they will say in that day: Are not these evils come upon us because our God is not among us?" (Deut. 31:17).

29. As was noted earlier, it is of particular interest to compare the same commentary's writings on the Bible and when the passage is quoted in the Talmud. Rashi made no comment on Prov. 3:6, yet he does expound it in his commentary on the Talmud.

30. A temporary suspension of a Torah law for some greater good.

31. My maternal grandfather, Hermann Stern, of blessed memory, fought in the German Army during World War I. The German Chief Rabbinate disseminated a ruling that Jewish soldiers were permitted to eat the non-kosher rations, thus violating a Torah law, since not eating would put their lives at risk all the more in combat conditions.

32. See *Sanhedrin* 4b-5a.

33. Perhaps stealing is approved in some cases, for example stealing food to feed one's family, or stealing expensive medicine to cure a sick relative.

Chapter 5

Pleasantness and Peace

תלמוד בבלי גיטין נט עמוד א

מתני': אלו דברים אמרו מפני דרכי שלום: כהן קורא ראשון ואחריו לוי ואחריו ישראל, מפני דרכי שלום... גמ': מנה"מ?... תנא דבי רבי ישמעאל: "וקדשתו" לכל דבר שבקדושה, לפתוח ראשון, ולברך ראשון, וליטול מנה יפה ראשון. א"ל אביי לרב יוסף: מפני דרכי שלום? דאורייתא היא! א"ל: דאורייתא, ומפני דרכי שלום. כל התורה כולה נמי מפני דרכי שלום היא, דכתי': "דרכיה דרכי נועם וכל נתיבותיה שלום"!

Gittin 59a-b

Mishnah: The following rules were laid down in the interests of peace. A *kohen* is called up first to read the law, and after him a Levi and then an Israelite in the interests of peace.... Gemara: What is the biblical textual source for this? ... A Tanna of the school of R. Yishmael taught, "And you shall sanctify him [the *kohen*]" (Lev. 21:8), [give him precedence] in all matters of holiness, to open proceedings, to say grace first, and to choose his portion first. Said Abaye to R. Joseph: Is this rule only [a rabbinic one] in the interests of peace [*darkhei shalom*]? Doesn't it derive from the Torah [since it is based on a biblical verse]?

He [R. Joseph] answered: It does derive from the Torah, but its object is to maintain peace. And the whole of the Law is also for the purpose of promoting peace, as it is written, "Her ways are ways of pleasantness and all her paths are peace" (Prov. 3:17).[1]

A Different Verse in Proverbs

Chapter 4 discussed Bar Kappara's contention that the foundation of the Torah is "in all your ways know Him" (Prov. 3:6). R. Joseph contends that a different verse in Proverbs is of central importance: "Her ways are ways of pleasantness and all her paths are peace" (Prov. 3:17). While R. Joseph's observation is made in the midst of a give-and-take regarding the basis for a ritual codified in the Mishnah, rather than an independent statement,[2] that should not deter us from accepting that R. Joseph thought this specific verse was central to the entire Torah.

Thus I am disagreeing with R. Walter Wurzburger, who wrote:

> There is no indication whatsoever in the Talmudic passage cited, that "the ways of peace" represent the ultimate aim and overall objective of the Torah. The texts in question really emphasize that "the ways of peace" represent one of the numerous features characterizing the precepts of the Torah. There is no evidence whatsoever that these characteristics constitute any more than merely pragmatically useful consequences which ensue in the wake of living in accordance with the precepts of the

Torah. The text, however, does not provide any support for the contention that the very purpose of the Torah is to bring about conditions of peace and pleasantness.[3]

In my opinion, R. Joseph's assertion should not merely be viewed as a side comment uttered in the heat of debate, but as the basis of a candidate for the point of the entirety of Jewish religious observance.

Comparing Prov. 3:6 and Prov. 3:17
We can distinguish between the two basic ideas derived from Proverbs 3. Bar Kappara's verse relates to the type of belief that underlies the Torah; he emphasizes that knowledge of God should be the focal point of all human activity. Alternatively, R. Joseph's statement says that the Torah and all of its commandments are defined by the traits of pleasantness and peace. Bar Kappara focuses on a cognitive[4] dimension of the observant life, in contrast to R. Joseph, who is concerned with one's emotional composition when complying with the Torah's commandments.[5] Consequently, we do not have to view the two verses as in disagreement with one another. Rather, Bar Kappara and R. Joseph may reflect complementary perspectives concerning basic dimensions of Judaism.

"Pleasantness" and "Peace" in Prov. 3:17
This verse has two key terms, *noam* (pleasantness) and *shalom* (peace), and it should be clear that these two words do not mean the same thing. First of all, the word "peace" is more objective and easier to define than "pleasantness." Second, the word *shalom* is considered one of the secondary names of God (a *kinnui*), unlike

noam (see *Shabbat* 10b). The word *shalom* is used as an appellation of God because the root of *shalom* is the same as *shalem*, which means "whole."[6] Third, *shalom* is superior to *noam*, since the oft-used rabbinic phrase is *darkhei shalom*, "ways of peace,"[7] based on this verse (assuming the phrase is not an abbreviated form of *darkhei shalom ve-noam*). The term *darkhei shalom* is used in some social contexts to obligate behavior that otherwise would not have been required.

One of the reasons "peace" is easier to define than "pleasantness" is that the former is used much more frequently in biblical texts,[8] rabbinic literature,[9] as well as standard Jewish liturgy. Consider the following examples:

Bible:
Speak unto Aaron and unto his sons, saying: "In this way you shall bless the children of Israel; you shall say unto them: The Lord bless you, and keep you; The Lord make His face to shine upon you, and be gracious unto you; the Lord lift up His countenance upon you, and give you peace (Num. 6:23-26).

Rabbinic literature:
R. Eleazar said in the name of R. Chanina: The disciples of the wise increase peace in the world, as it says, "And all your children shall be knowledgeable of the Lord, and great shall be the peace of your children" (Isa. 54:13). Read not *banayikh* [your children] but *bonayikh* [your builders]. "Great peace have they that love Your Law, and there is no stumbling for them" (Ps. 119:165). "Peace be within your walls and prosperity within your palaces. For

my brethren and companions' sake I will now say, peace be within you. For the sake of the house of the Lord our God I will seek your good" (Ps. 122:7-9). "The Lord will give strength unto His people, the Lord will bless His people with peace" (Ps. 29:11) (*Berakhot* 64a).

When two people quarreled, Aaron went and sat down with one of them and said to him, "My son, know that your friend has said, 'I am ashamed before him because I have sinned against him.'" Aaron would sit with him until he had dispelled the ill-feeling from his heart. Then Aaron would go and sit with the other one and say to him, "Know that your friend is saying, 'Woe is to me! How shall I raise my eyes and look at my friend? I am ashamed before him because I have sinned against him.'" Aaron would sit with him until he had dispelled the ill-feeling from his heart. When the two friends later met, they embraced and kissed each other. There were thousands in Israel who were called by the name "Aaron," for if not for Aaron, they would not have come into the world. Aaron made peace between husband and wife so that they came together, and they named the child that was born after him (*Avot de-Rabbi Natan* 12:3).

Liturgical texts:
Grant peace, goodness and blessing, grace, loving kindness and compassion, to us and all Israel Your people. Bless us, our Father, all as one, with the light of Your face, for by the light of Your face, You have given us, Lord our God, the Torah of life and the love of kindness, righteousness,

blessing and compassion, life and peace. May it be good in Your eyes to bless Your people Israel at every time, in every hour, with Your peace. Blessed are You, Lord, Who blesses His people Israel with peace (end of *Shacharit Amidah*).

May He Who makes peace in His high places, make peace for us and all Israel—and say, "Amen" (*Kaddish*).

Consequently, it can be maintained that Judaism views peace as an overall objective that should ideally inform the dynamics of all our endeavors: *shalom bayit*[10] stresses peace between husband and wife, *hava'at shalom bein ish le-chaveiro* emphasizes peace between quarrelling neighbors,[11] and *ha-mattil shalom bein… umma le-umma, bein memshalah le-memshalah* teaches how important it is for God to make peace between peoples and nations. It is therefore not surprising that peace is the state of affairs that will characterize the messianic period, which according to Jewish tradition is the ultimate goal of human history (see Isa. 11:1-9 and Maimonides, *Melakhim* 12:2, 5).

In contrast, "pleasantness" is more ephemeral and difficult to define precisely. There are only three talmudic passages where "pleasantness" is held up as a desirable virtue:

Abaye explained: As it was taught, "And you shall love the Lord your God" (Deut. 6:5) — that the Name of Heaven be beloved because of you. If someone studies Scripture and Mishnah, and waits on the disciples of the wise, is honest in business, and speaks pleasantly to persons, what do people then say concerning him? "Happy is the father who taught him Torah, happy is the teacher who taught him Torah; woe unto people who have not studied the Torah; for this man who has studied the Torah, look how fine his ways are, how righteous his deeds!" Of him does Scripture say, "And He said unto me: 'You are My servant, Israel, in whom I will be glorified'" (Isa. 49:3).

But if someone studies Scripture and Mishnah, waits on the disciples of the wise, but is dishonest in business, and discourteous in his relations with people, what do people say about him? "Woe unto him who studied the Torah, woe unto his father who taught him Torah; woe unto his teacher who taught him Torah! This man studied the Torah: Look, how corrupt are his deeds, how ugly his ways." Of him Scripture says, "In that men said of them: 'These are the people of the Lord, and are gone forth out of His Land'" (Ezek. 36:20) (*Yoma* 86a).

R. Ashi said: A scholar who is not as hard as iron is no scholar, as it is said, "And like a hammer that breaks the rock in pieces" (Jer. 23:29). R. Abba said to R. Ashi: You have learned this from that verse, but we have learned it from the following verse, "A land whose stones are iron" (Deut. 8:9). Do not read, *avaneha* [her stones] but *boneha* [her builders].

Ravina said: Despite this, a man should train himself to be pleasant, for it is said, "Therefore remove vexation from thy heart" (Eccl. 11:10) (*Ta'anit* 4a).

R. Oshia said: What is the meaning of the verse, "And I took unto me the two staves; the one I called *noam* [pleasantness] and the other I called *chovlim* [binders]" (Zech. 11:7)? — *Noam* refers to the scholars of Palestine, who treat each other pleasantly [*man'imim*] when engaged in halakhic debates. *Chovlim* to the scholars of Babylon, who injure each other's feelings [*mechablim*] when discussing *halakhah* (*Sanhedrin* 24a).

All three of these sources are addressing scholars who may become overly impressed with themselves to the point of arrogance and insensitivity. The Rabbis were aware that the same individuals who possess the greatest understanding of Torah and *mitzvot* might also be most susceptible to missing a basic point of the Jewish tradition. Perhaps this is why the Torah goes out of its way to emphasize the humility of both Abraham and Moses.[12] Despite, or perhaps specifically because of, their awareness of their closeness to God, they recognized their smallness compared to the Divine, a recognition which allowed their dealings with others to be exemplary and proper.[13]

Even scholars require reminders of what is truly important with respect to their considerable learning and mastery of the contents of Jewish tradition. Nobody, not even a scholar, is immune from becoming arrogant, and they are not entitled to assume that pleasantness and peace will automatically shape their sensibilities, no matter how much Torah they know or how many *mitzvot* they fulfill. It stands to reason that if Torah scholars must be punctilious about maintaining a proper attitude towards others, this should all the more be the case with those who have not reached such lofty spiritual heights.

The Great Principle of the Torah

Are Torah and *Mitzvot* Transformative?

One Midrash understands Prov. 3:17 as defining not only the essence of the *mitzvot* of the Torah, but also a prerequisite that qualifies human beings to receive the Torah in the first place:

> "Her ways are ways of pleasantness and all her paths are peace" (Prov. 3:17): The Holy One, blessed be He, wished to give the Torah at the moment the Jews left Egypt. But they were fighting with one another, as it says, "And they journeyed [*va-yisu* (plural)] from Succot and they encamped [*va-yachanu*] in Etam, on the edge of the wilderness" (Exod. 13:20). They travelled in strife and encamped in strife. Only after their stay in Rephidim were they unified and became a single unit, as it says, "And when they journeyed [*va-yisu*] from Rephidim, and they came [*va-yavo'u*] to the wilderness of Sinai, they encamped [*va-yachanu*] in the wilderness; and there Israel encamped [*va-yichan* (singular)] before the mount" (Exod. 19:2). It does not say *va-yachanu*. Said the Holy One, blessed be He: The Torah is completely a manifestation of peace. And to whom will I give it? To a nation that loves peace. This is why the verse states, "and all her paths are peace" (*Yalkut Shimoni, Mishlei* 934).

This source suggests a specific viewpoint regarding the "nurture-nature" question as it applies to the practice of *mitzvot*. According to this Midrash, an individual or an entire nation must be at peace before it can appreciate the Torah and its *mitzvot*.

One could alternatively contend that by means of practicing *mitzvot*, one's essential nature is altered, and thereby reaches a form of higher consciousness and spiritual sensitivity, regardless of where one starts out. The *Sefer ha-Chinnukh* notes repeatedly the assumption that by engaging in external actions, over time one internalizes the values inherent in those actions:

> You should know that a human being is affected by his actions, and his heart and all of his thoughts follow the actions in which he is engaged, whether for good or bad. [This applies to] even someone who is completely evil in his heart, i.e., "… And all the thoughts of his heart were only evil continually" (Gen. 6:5). If his spirit becomes awakened and he directs his efforts and activities to steadfastly engage in Torah and *mitzvot*, even if for ulterior motives, immediately he will be influenced for good, and by means of his actions he will slay his evil inclination, because the heart is drawn after one's external actions. And even if he is a completely righteous individual and his heart is upright and pure, desirous of fulfilling Torah and *mitzvot*, if he comes to always engage in inconsequential matters [he will change for the worse]. As a parable, if the king would appoint him to fulfill a responsibility involving an evil craft, surely by his constant daily involvement in that activity, he will over time change from his previous righteousness to become a completely evil individual, for it is known and it is true that every person is influenced by his actions, as we have said.
>
> Therefore the Sages, may their memory be for a blessing, said, "God wished to benefit Israel. For this reason He increased for them Torah and *mitzot*" (*Makkot* 23b)[14] in order to form all of our thoughts and for all of our

activities to be devoted to them, to cause good to come to us in the end, because as a result of our good actions, we are influenced to be good and to be deserving of the life in the World to Come. And the Rabbis hinted regarding this idea when they said, "Whoever has a *mezuzah* on his doorway and *tzitzit* on his garment and *tefillin* on his head is assured that he will not sin, because these are constant commandments and he will be affected by them constantly..." (*Menachot* 43b) (*Sefer ha-Chinnukh, Mitzvah* 16).

The *Chinnukh* believes that commandments are intended to alter an individual's personality, and that his personality can be changed, even if at first he is completely evil in his heart. Based on this, there is no prerequisite for being righteous or noble in order to receive the Torah. Instead, the Torah itself and the commandments will refine the individual's character.

Essentially the question becomes: is the Torah intended to be transformative, to change the basic essence of people from neutral to holy, or is it intended solely for those who already possess positive qualities to refine them and make them even better? The truth likely rests somewhere in the middle, and we can adopt the position that while certain qualities must exist even prior to study and performing *mitzvot*, these activities can take him to an even higher level than he would have been able to achieve otherwise.

Rav Joseph's Motivation

We can view R. Joseph's comment in several ways. First, we can analyze his general approach to textual interpretation. Second, we can see what writings exist about his personality, and how that might have led him to identify this as the central idea of Judaism. Third, we can also explore the events that occurred in his life, and the personal experiences that could have influenced his behavior. These all may enable us to better understand why he advocated Prov. 3:17 as the fundamental principle of the Torah, to the exclusion of all other texts.

R. Joseph made numerous derivations from biblical sources of general rules, principles, and solutions to questions, very much paralleling his comment regarding Prov. 3:17.

Dr. Mordechai Margoliot[15] writes:

> Many times he would explain things [in rabbinic tradition based upon biblical verses], and the following formula appears often in the Talmud: "From where does this [law, ritual, etc.] come from? Said R. Joseph...."[16]

However, R. Joseph's interest in Prov. 3:17 may not have been exclusively due to his general methodological approach looking to link the written and oral traditions. When Dr. Margoliot discusses R. Joseph's personal attributes he adds:[17]

> R. Joseph's extreme humility was well-known, as stated at the end of *Sotah*.[18] And when he would make an error, he would admit his mistake publicly.[19]

If R. Joseph had a strong sense of ethics and morality, it would not be surprising for him to project such sensibilities upon the Torah. If pleasantness and peace were key values for R. Joseph, he would more likely view the entire Torah through such a lens.

R. Joseph at one point suffered a serious illness which resulted in his forgetting all of the Torah that he had mastered, and requiring his student Abaye to reteach the material to him.[20] He also lost his sight permanently.[21] One can imagine that this condition resulted in his having to depend upon many acts of kindness by others in order for him to function, which would have formed his perspective on Torah. He experienced first-hand how crucial kindness, pleasantness, and peace were, and he came to the conclusion that God, through His Torah, would encourage and command people to help others, as one of the main objectives of Judaism.

These various factors—methodological preferences, personal attributes, and a major handicap—beg the question whether someone who did not have R. Joseph's experience would have approached the Torah in the same manner. But on another level, despite R. Joseph's personal difficulties, it is important to consider whether his perspective has merit as a universal principle, not something merely derived from his individual circumstances.

The Uniqueness of Prov. 3:17

The virtues of pleasantness and peace are universally acknowledged as central to not only the quality of Jewish life, but human life in general. If human beings are meant to function best in social settings (as discussed earlier), then it is clearly desirable for each person to interact positively with others, and without conflict or strife. Much of human frustration and suffering could be obviated if pleasantness and peace were higher priorities for people. If such an ideal is optimal in general, then it is reasonable to expect religious activities to also promote a sense of positive personal satisfaction and the avoidance of hostility. Yet one is struck by the fact that there are no biblical texts that explicitly associate pleasantness and peace with Torah and *mitzvot* other than Prov. 3:17!

Pleasantness and Peace

Only a single verse in Psalms, and even then, only according to two commentators, associates Torah with pleasantness. In Psalm 27:4, David wistfully articulates an ideal that is illusive for any busy religious individual, let alone a king:

> One thing have I asked of the Lord, that will I seek after: that I may dwell in the House of the Lord all the days of my life, to behold the pleasantness of God [*noam Hashem*], and to visit early in His Temple.

Rabbi David Altshuler, in his *Metzudat David*, explains: "to see [*la-chazot*]: to see the pleasantness of God's Torah [*li-rot be-ne'imut torat Hashem*]." In other words, King David is lamenting that he does not have enough time to study and reflect upon Torah traditions and commandments which articulate "pleasantness" and by which he is called upon not only to conduct his own life, but also to reference as a template for governing his kingdom.[22]

R. Samson Raphael Hirsch[23] develops a similar idea, but instead of attributing to David a desire to study Torah, Rabbi Hirsch discusses the symbolism associated with certain objects in the tabernacle and Temple, specifically the Ark containing the whole and broken tablets,[24] as well as a Torah scroll written by Moses.[25] Since the king witnesses the Ark, along with its contents, when he visits the house of the Lord, David realizes how important it is for him to visit as often as possible:

> *Noam* is that which is attractive, pleasant, satisfying or blissful. It is difficult to express the meaning properly by any one word. Thus the ways of life taught us by Divine wisdom are referred to as *darkhei noam* (Prov. 3:17). *Noam*

Hashem (Ps. 27:4) is the blissfully glorious way in which the Lord shapes human affairs on earth in accordance with His purposes. This *noam Hashem* has its concrete embodiment in the Devir,[26] the Holy of Holies in the Temple. There the Ark of the Law reposes, guarded by the cherubim with wings outspread over the Ark to protect it.[27] At the same time the wings of these supernatural beings point upward as if to receive God's glory. It is this Ark that demonstrates to us that wherever God's Law is observed with genuine, pure determination and to an ever-increasing degree, there all of earthly existence will become the bearer of the Divine here and below and will attain the presence of the glory of the Lord on earth…. The Torah, reposing in the Holy of Holies, lights our lamp, prepares our table, grants us the physical means for life on earth and the spiritual prerequisites for life eternal, and at the same time teaches us how to devote all our physical and spiritual energies to the fulfillment of the will of the Lord on earth… (s.v., *la-chazot*).

R. Hirsch expresses a noble sentiment that the Torah, which can be appreciated by one's emotions rather than one's mind, is meant to spiritually prepare us for the physical world. To the extent that the quality of pleasantness is associated with God Himself, and engendered by thinking about the contents of the Torah which He gave to the Jewish people, this explanation of Ps. 27:4 could be viewed as conforming with R. Joseph's interpretation of Prov. 3:17.

Just as one would struggle to locate biblical verses that speak of the Torah's pleasantness, there are virtually no verses that equate the commandments with the qualities of peace. R. Joseph may have felt drawn to Prov. 3:17 because, out of the 237 times that the word *shalom* is used in the Hebrew Bible,[28] only one other verse associates peace with even some of the commandments:

> These are the things that you shall do: Speak every man the truth with his neighbor; execute the judgment of truth and peace [*shalom*] in your gates (Zech. 8:16).

The verse in Zechariah is limited, at best addressing only interpersonal commandments in general, and, if we read the end of the verse narrowly, only those specific laws that will be handled by judges. In contrast, Prov. 3:17 makes a statement regarding the entirety of the Torah's contents, including interpersonal commandments, as well as those between man and God, and it concerns all of the commandments, whether or not they are adjudicated by judges. While it is readily understandable how laws that make up the social contract of a society should generate peace and harmony among its citizens, it is intriguing to speculate how the desire for peace influences commandments between man and God.

Chapter 2 discussed Ben Azzai's opinion that the central theme of Judaism is "this is the book of the generations of man" (Gen. 5:1). The *Korban ha-Edah* understood Ben Azzai to say that developing a sensitivity to God should result in greater kindness and consideration for all of humanity, since each person is created in God's image, regardless of the differences that exist between philosophies, theologies, and practices. This may be R. Joseph's opinion as well, in elevating Prov. 3:17 as the highest value: appreciation of the Torah and its contents will prioritize pleasantness and peace above all values.

The Great Principle of the Torah

Does Religion Create Peace?

In an op-ed article in the *New York Times* (July 19, 2014), entitled "Faith-Based Fanatics," Timothy Egan noted, counterintuitively I would add, that in the three-volume *Encyclopedia of Wars*, wherein 1723 conflicts are recorded, only 123 wars (less than 7%) were due to religious strife. In other words, according to Egan, the institution of religion has historically not been one of the greatest causes of armed conflict. One could even say that religion historically has promoted pleasantness and peace more than it has caused war.

Does Religion Create Inner Peace?

Proverbs 3:17 can also be saying that the *kavanah* (intention or mindfulness) should be for peace and pleasantness when performing *mitzvot*. The Sages stress that each commandment should be performed *lishmah* (for its own sake, and not for reward). Perhaps part of this teaching means that each *mitzvah* should convey a sense of pleasantness and peace when it is properly fulfilled. Hence performing more *mitzvot* properly can increase peace in the world. Perhaps the fact that no verses aside from Prov. 3:17 suggest such an approach reflects how difficult it is to achieve this aspiration. While we have referenced Rabbi Aharon Lichtenstein that the Torah promotes a culture of aspiration (see Chapter 3), perhaps this ideal is viewed by even God as so extreme, that aside from a single biblical reference, it would not be explicitly promulgated as part of the Jewish written tradition.

Is R. Joseph Realistic?

Jewish history has clearly demonstrated that there are times when we cannot assume that everything will always be informed by pleasantness and peace. When an enemy attacks you, either individually or as a nation, if you are to survive, you will have to defend yourself. In those cases, there is a commandment to engage in self-defense. As Ecclesiastes states, "A time to love, and a time to hate; a time for war, and a time for peace" (Eccl. 3:8).

Furthermore, every religious system—and in this Judaism is no exception—inevitably delineates categories of "heretics" who, due to their rejection of some fundamental theological premise that the religion considers inviolable, are deemed deserving of eradication. Can aspirations for ideological purity go hand-in-hand with calls for pleasantness and peace? Is it possible to compartmentalize, to generally embrace pleasantness and peace as overriding values, but nevertheless to assume a judgmental and even militant stance towards those deemed as undermining the fabric of the religion?

Additionally, there are the numerous Torah rules that either exclude or at least severely limit the rights and activities of certain individuals due to their gender, beliefs, or social status.[29] The hierarchical nature implicit in the Torah may benefit those who occupy the highest places of status and honor, for whom observing the *mitzvot* comes without sacrifice. But what about individuals who are excluded by the Torah's laws? Will they think of the Jewish tradition as the repository of pleasantness and peace?

Is R. Joseph Wrong?
Maybe R. Joseph is wrong. There are times military action is necessary, there are times when we need to take strong stands against those who reject basic Jewish beliefs and values, and there are some people who suffer personally or socially, or feel outcast. There will probably be many Jews and non-Jews who would not agree that the Torah's ways engender pleasantness and peace.

Ben Zoma taught, "Who is wealthy? He who is satisfied with his lot" (*Avot* 4:1). Obviously, humility, lack of covetousness, and a general positive attitude are commendable traits. It is also clear that Ben Zoma is not just speaking about material wealth. For example, the *Ketav ve-ha-Kabbalah*, commenting on the verse, "And also that nation, whom they shall serve, will I judge; and afterward shall they come out with great sustenance" (Gen. 15:14), writes the following:

> Every intelligent individual necessarily understands that the acquisition of money was not the intended purpose of the servitude [in Egypt], for would a person willingly undergo affliction and servitude in order to obtain a significant sum afterwards? Wouldn't he be likely to say, "[Neither from] your sting nor from your honey"... so we are compelled to say... that without a doubt the acquisition of substance for the soul was the intended goal of the servitude... to purify them from all of the ritual impurity in order to purify their souls by removing all false beliefs, and via the signs and wonders that were performed in Egypt on their behalves, there would be publicized the truth of His Existence, His involvement in human affairs and His omnipotence...

Nonetheless, Ben Zoma's teaching seems to be about material and perhaps even spiritual wealth. It does not seem to address halakhic categories that are imposed externally, to make someone's situation worse. Ben Zoma's statement does not seem to imply that someone should be satisfied that an external halakhic system creates categories that marginalize or disenfranchise certain people.

Furthermore, it is very difficult to reach a constant state of peace and satisfaction, even for someone who is not negatively affected by the halakhic process. Jacob was the only person in the Bible called *shalem*, "whole," and only for a short period of time (see p. 183 note 6). It is very difficult for anyone to achieve, and harder to sustain, a sense of peace and pleasantness over the course of a lifetime.

When Someone Feels Rejected by Religion
Two accounts in the Bible exemplify how conflict and strife can result from the Torah and its hierarchical structure. The first is the blasphemer (*mekallel*), and the second is Korach. When individuals perceive and experience Jewish law and its application as decidedly unpleasant because of what they consider personal deprivations, terrible consequences often result.

The first is the case of the blasphemer:

> A man whose mother was an Israelite and whose father was an Egyptian came out among the people of Israel; and the Israelite woman's son and a certain Israelite began fighting in the camp. The Israelite woman's son blasphemed the Name in a curse. And they brought him to Moses—now his mother's name was Shelomith, daughter of Dibri, of the tribe of Dan—and they put him in custody, until the decision of the Lord should be made clear to them. The Lord said to Moses, saying: Take the blasphemer outside the camp; and let all who were within hearing lay their hands on his head, and let the whole congregation stone him. And speak to the people of Israel, saying: Anyone who curses God shall bear the sin. One

who blasphemes the name of the Lord shall be put to death; the whole congregation shall stone the blasphemer. Aliens as well as citizens, when they blaspheme the Name, shall be put to death. Anyone who kills a human being shall be put to death. Anyone who kills an animal shall make restitution for it, life for life. Anyone who maims another shall suffer the same injury in return: fracture for fracture, eye for eye, tooth for tooth; the injury inflicted is the injury to be suffered. One who kills an animal shall make restitution for it; but one who kills a human being shall be put to death. You shall have one law for the alien and for the citizen: for I am the Lord your God. Moses spoke thus to the people of Israel; and they took the blasphemer outside the camp, and stoned him to death. The people of Israel did as the Lord had commanded Moses (Lev. 24:10-23).

There is no question that this individual transgressed grievously, undermining the reverence that people should feel towards God. Flaunting disdain for the Divine encourages others to think similar thoughts, leading to disregarding the rules and decrees that organize religious society and are designed to inspire man to become more Godly—pleasant and peaceful—himself. As evidence of the centrality of this transgression, not only are Jews enjoined against blaspheming, but even non-Jews are expected to comply with this stricture, since it constitutes one of the seven Noahide laws.[30]

Of more immediate interest is to ask what drove this individual to publicly blaspheme in the first place. He was fighting with another individual—but not every altercation automatically escalates to blasphemy. The Rabbis wondered about this as well, and cite three possible catalysts for the man's actions, all relying on the word *va-yeitzei*, "[and he] went out" at the beginning of this passage (Lev. 24:10).

First, R. Levi said *va-yeitzei* means he "went out" of this world by committing the capital crime of blasphemy. Second. R. Berechiah says he "went out" (went astray) from respecting the Torah. The third opinion, belonging to R. Chiya, is of greatest consequence to us, since he expresses how someone who feels ostracized may come to commit blasphemy:

> R. Chiya taught: He went out from the matter of genealogical relationships, for he came to pitch his tent among the encampment of the tribe of Dan. He said to them, "I am related to the daughters of Dan" (cf. Lev. 24:11). They said to him: But it is written, "The children of Israel shall pitch [their tents] adjacent to their fathers' houses; every man with his own standard, according to the ensigns; a good way off shall they pitch round about the tent of meeting" (Num. 2:2). [His father was not Jewish, so he didn't have a tribe.] He went to the court of Moses and he left with the pronouncement that his claim was not valid. He stood and blasphemed... (*Yalkut Shimoni, Parashat Emor* 657).

According to R. Chiya, this individual, through no fault of his own, found himself disenfranchised. And since these laws are divine, he blamed God directly for his unhappiness. However, just because he was unhappy was not sufficient reason to engage in such drastic measures, actions which ultimately resulted in his demise. Even though we might say the blasphemer overreacted, it should also be clear that he did not believe the Torah promotes the values of "pleasantness" and "peace."

One could make a similar claim regarding Korach. Once again the Rabbis explain what motivated him to lead a challenge against human and Divine authority:

> Now Korach son of Izhar son of Kohath son of Levi, along with Dathan and Abiram sons of Eliab, and On son of Peleth—descendants of Reuben—took two hundred and fifty Israelite men, leaders of the congregation, chosen from the assembly, well-known men, and they confronted Moses. They assembled against Moses and against Aaron, and said to them, "You have gone too far! All the congregation are holy, every one of them, and the Lord is among them. So why then do you exalt yourselves above the assembly of the Lord?" (Num. 16:1-3).

Rashi explains the nature of Korach's discontent:

> … And what caused Korach to enter into dispute with Moses? He was jealous of the position of prince that had been assigned to Elitzafan ben Uziel, whom Moses appointed to be in charge of the family of Kohath, in accordance with the Divine decree. Said Korach: My father had four brothers, as it is written, "And the sons of Kohath: Amram, Izhar, Hebron, and Uzziel. And the years of the life of Kohath were a hundred thirty and three years" (Exod. 6:18). Amram, the first-born, his two sons were appointed to high positions, one the king [Moses]

and one the High Priest [Aaron]. Who is worthy of the next most important position? Shouldn't it be me, because I am the son of Izhar, who was second-born after Amram? And instead he [Moses] appointed as leader [*nasi*] the son of the youngest of the brothers [Uzziel]! I will challenge him and will refute his words... (Rashi on Num. 16:1, s.v. *ve-Datan ve-Aviram*).

Korach believed that Moses had made the decision of leadership himself, and refused to accept that it was God who had made the appointment. In the view of Korach, Moses was discriminating against him, under the guise of authentic Torah leadership.

Since the Torah does not assign equal status to everyone, the individual who feels spurned might experience jealousy, resentment, and ultimately alienation. This is especially true if someone believes it was not the Torah itself that imposed the law, but a human authority with personal biases, which is exactly what Korach claimed. However, many issues are not decided by individual merit, but based on some esoteric Divine concern.[31] Since many of these judgments are predetermined, is it possible for Jewish leaders to conduct their lives by the values of pleasantness and peace?

Ultimately, R. Joseph's opinion may constitute an idea that is far from reality, and therefore requires innovative interpretation.

How Do We Respond to This Frustration?

Certainly one could dismiss Korach as irrelevant to our discussion. We could condemn him by saying he possessed an obsessive hunger for power. We could claim he didn't even take his own claim seriously, and that he only used it as a guise for his self-aggrandizement. There may always be people who cannot fully appreciate the Torah's values, and perhaps Korach was one of them.

But another way to view Korach, as well as the blasphemer, is to see them as similar to ourselves. We all have desires and expectations that do not materialize, dreams that have gone unfulfilled. We all have entertained feelings of jealousy towards others who appear to have been endowed with abilities, capacities, and opportunities that we have not enjoyed. While these inequities are largely beyond our control, nevertheless how we choose to respond is our personal responsibility. Perhaps this is at least in part what R. Chanina meant when he said, "Everything is in the hands of Heaven except for the fear of Heaven" (*Berakhot* 33b). In other words, each of us is dealt a certain hand over which we have no control. The blasphemer could not choose his parents, and Korach could not attain the leadership position he coveted.

All that is left is how we respond to the reality in which we find ourselves, particularly in relation to God. Do we blame God for what we consider an injury or oversight, or do we accept our situations, viewing them as personal challenges to see how we can best maximize what we can achieve, given the circumstances, and even judge our situation as potentially pleasant on some level, and ultimately a manifestation of true peace. This is particularly true for the word *shalom*, which derives from *shalem*, which means "whole." R. Joseph was far from whole. He was afflicted with a condition that made him forget all of his learning. He was also blind. Yet he was able to say that the key verse in the Bible is, "its ways are ways of pleasantness and all its paths are peace." Is it possible that our individual challenges are the key to realizing a sense of wholeness, not in comparison to others or even to God, but in terms of who each of us is individually?

Pleasantness and Peace

How the Talmud Uses This Verse

In several talmudic passages, Prov. 3:17 is cited to reach conclusions in specific discussions. Here are three examples where this verse served to resolve a difficulty:

Case 1 (*Sukkah* 32a-b)

The Torah requires one to wave four species for the holiday of Sukkot, but does not clearly specify which species are required: "And you shall take on the first day the fruit of goodly trees, branches of palm-trees, and boughs of thick trees, and willows of the brook, and you shall rejoice before the Lord your God seven days" (Lev. 23:40). One suggestion in the Talmud is for a species that has spikes on it:

> But perhaps it means the inflorescence [including spikes] of palms? Abaye answered: It is written, "Her ways are ways of pleasantness, and all her paths are peace...." Our Rabbis taught, "Boughs of a thick tree" — whose branches completely cover its trunk. Now what is this? Obviously you must say that it is the myrtle.... But perhaps it is the oleander [which is thick but also poisonous]? Abaye said, "Her ways are the ways of pleasantness," and [with the oleander] this is not the case (*Sukkah* 32a-b).

Case 2 (*Yevamot* 87b)

If a married man dies childless, his surviving brother has the mitzvah of *yibbum* or *chalitzah*. *Yibbum* is when the surviving brother marries the widow; *chalitzah* is when the surviving brother performs a ritual akin to divorce to permanently sever the connection between the widow and the brother's family (see Deut. 25:5-10). The Talmud presents the following case: The husband dies but there is a surviving child (so there is no *yibbum*), and then she remarries. However, once she is remarried, the child from her first marriage dies. Should *yibbum* now apply retroactively? If yes, this would require her current marriage to be dissolved.

A related question is as follows: A *bat kohen* (daughter of a *kohen*) can eat *terumah* (one of the priestly gifts) as long as she lives in her father's home. Once she gets married, if she marries a non-*kohen*, she is no longer allowed to eat *terumah*. However, if she is widowed without children, she may return to her home and eat *terumah*. If she is widowed but has a surviving child, she may not eat *terumah*. However, if her child then dies, is she allowed to eat *terumah*? The Talmud addresses these questions:

> Said Rav Yehudah of Diskarta to Rava: The dead should not be given the same status as the living regarding levirate marriage, by inference *a minori ad majus*:
>
> If where a child by the first husband is regarded as the child of the second husband, in respect of disqualifying the woman from eating *terumah*, the dead were not given the same status as the living, how much less should the dead be given the same status as the living where the child of the first husband is not regarded as the son of the second, with respect to exempting the woman from the levirate marriage! [Rava responds]: It was expressly stated, "Her ways are ways of pleasantness, and all her paths are peace" (*Yevamot* 87b).

Case 3 (Jerusalem Talmud *Eruvin* 3:2)

On Shabbat, one is not permitted to carry from one domain to another (Exod. 16:29). However, the Rabbis devised the concept of *eruv chatzerot* (literally, "mixing of courtyards") which in certain circumstances allows people to carry in areas that otherwise would have been forbidden. Sometimes the word "*eruv*" is also used to refer to the food that each family is required to contribute, thereby creating a single communal domain:

> Said R. Joshua: "Why are *eruvei chatzerot* made? Because of the interests of peace. A story about one woman who had a dispute with her colleague, and therefore sent her *eruv* [food contribution] with her son [instead of bringing it herself]. She [the neighbor] embraced him, hugged him and kissed him. He came back and told his mother what had happened. She said: How much she must love me and I was unaware. Because of this, they made peace with one another. This is what is meant when it is written, "Her ways are ways of pleasantness and all her paths are peace" (JT *Eruvin* 3:2).

Since the Rabbis invoked Prov. 3:17 to clarify ambiguous cases, perhaps R. Joseph was led to believe that the verse should be viewed as central to the Jewish halakhic tradition in general.

The Role of Prov. 3:17 in the Talmud

Perhaps none of these cases sufficiently validates R. Joseph's interpretation of Prov. 3:17. One could argue that the third case is not relevant at all, since it concerns an *eruv chatzerot*, which is rabbinic, not biblical, in nature. Furthermore, the first two cases—

the four species, and *yibbum*—do not use Prov. 3:17 as central to the case, but only as an afterthought. In other words, Prov. 3:17 is not included in the initial line of reasoning, but only mentioned at the end. Had Prov. 3:17 been used to explain why there is a commandment of the four species in the first place, or why the institution of *yibbum* increases societal harmony, that would have shown that these two *mitzvot* are rooted in pleasantness and peace.

In addition, there are some commandments that are viewed as concessions to man's baser instincts. Most notably are the *eshet yefat toar* (the "wife captive" of Deut. 21:10-14) and the blood-redeemer (Num. 35:22-28). These two institutions are permitted, even though they appeal to concupiscence and vengeance, respectively. Rashi says that the Torah is speaking in response to man's evil inclination (on Deut. 21:11, based on *Kiddushin* 21b). In these cases, the law seems less than ideal, but the Torah sanctions it, so to speak, to avoid some greater misfortune. Nonetheless, allowing man to succumb to his desires, and engage in these actions which are clearly detrimental to their victims, hardly seems in line with pleasantness and peace.

A Teleological Explanation

Perhaps R. Joseph never meant that each and every aspect of individual human life was supposed to be imbued with pleasantness and peace. As we have seen, the Torah has many laws that do not seem to promote peace. War, even in self-defense, is anything but peaceful, yet in certain circumstances war too is a commandment. The Torah creates certain social situations that seem to promote discord rather than pleasantness, like the case of the *mamzer*, *chalal*, and other classifications that seem exclusionary. And the most dramatic cases, the *eshet yefat toar* and the blood-redeemer, seem like concessions to man's baser instinct, with full disregard for the values of pleasantness and peace.

Perhaps R. Joseph only meant his statement to be understood in the messianic era, which will be characterized by peace and harmony, as opposed to this world, which has strife and discord. To this effect Rabbi Abraham Isaac Kook wrote that over the course of history, human values become more refined:

> The doctrine of evolution, which is presently gaining acceptance in the world, has a greater affinity with the secret teachings of Kabbalah than all other philosophies. Evolution, which proceeds on a course of improvement, offers us the basis for optimism in the world. How can we despair when we realize that everything evolves and improves? In probing the inner meaning of evolution toward an improved state, we find here an explanation of the Divine concepts with absolute clarity. It is precisely the *Ein Sof* [lit., "the One without end," i.e., God] in actuality that brings to realization the potentiality of *Ein Sof* (*Orot ha-Kodesh* II, p. 537).

For R. Kook, if slavery was once ubiquitous, even in the Western world, its rejection is cause for optimism regarding human nature. If women's rights have advanced, including in certain parts of the religious world, that is a positive development which draws us closer to the ultimate intent of the Creation. And a decrease in xenophobia and intolerance also marks a trend to ever greater peace and tranquility. While the short-term is often cause for pessimism about the state of the human race, adopting a long-range perspective offers a sense of how far humanity has come and can continue to positively evolve. Such a point of view could maintain that the Torah and its commandments will ultimately result in greater pleasantness and peace.

Implications for Contemporary Jews

First, the association between pleasantness and peace with Torah and *mitzvot* is a key idea that can encourage individuals to hold on to their religious beliefs and practices, as well as attract those seeking meaning and structure for their lives. While the human condition will always require one to do and experience things that are unpleasant and full of conflict, this should not be the overall or primary impression that religion and religious practices make upon people, whether they practice religion or not.

One could even argue that pleasantness and peace are the vectors that determine whether one is sanctifying or profaning God's name in public. A friend once said to me about another, "He wears his religion well." The manner in which this individual practiced religion was inspiring, consistent, ennobling, humane, and elegant. This is the ideal mentioned in the Talmud above, "Happy is the father who taught him Torah, happy is the teacher who taught him Torah; woe unto people who have not studied the Torah; for this man who has studied the Torah, look how fine his ways are, how righteous his deeds" (*Yoma* 86a). Consequently, when the Torah and its practices are studied, taught, and promulgated, emphasis should be placed on how these teachings and lifestyle contribute pleasantness and peace with both Jews and non-Jews, as well as to one's personal sense of well-being.

The following story is told in the name of Rabbi Moshe Feinstein, about how one should view the Torah as valuable and pleasant, rather than burdensome:

Pleasantness and Peace

The sagacious Rabbi Moshe Feinstein was asked once: It is well-known that the Jews who emigrated from Europe to America two or three generations ago endured exceedingly great hardships in order to properly observe Shabbat. It was said about many of them that they worked in fifty-two places a year, since at the end of each Friday, they were fired from their jobs because of their desire to keep Shabbat. How then did it happen that the great majority the children of these God-fearing and suffering Jews [*mosrei nefesh*] completely abandoned religion, and they are not Shabbat observant at all?

Rav Moshe responded that it is precisely because they suffered [*masru nefesh*] for Shabbat. Therefore their children didn't keep Shabbat at all! How is this so? Rather, those Jews who suffered to keep Shabbat committed a significant error in judgment. When they would come home from the difficult ordeal they experienced, they expressed sadness and bitter disappointment that they were forced to leave their jobs for the sake of Shabbat. Their children absorbed the feeling that observing Shabbat in America requires inordinate sacrifice, difficulty, and anguish, and concluded from this that they could not endure this type of suffering, and it would be better for them to abandon Shabbat.

It would not have been this way if their parents had come home and announced joyfully, "Thank God that we have merited once again to keep Shabbat properly. How happy we are, and how good is our portion to have withstood this test." Then their children would have inherited from them the joy and happiness of keeping the commandments. Who does not want to be joyous and make others joyous as well? They too would have been willing to observe it with the same commitment [*mesirat nefesh*], in joyfulness and goodheartedness.[32]

Naturally there will be situations where taking a strict position on a halakhic matter is required. As a result, there will always be people who feel that religious law has been insensitively applied. It is necessary for the Jewish leaders to make absolutely certain that before they make a pronouncement that could have negative social consequences, they have exhausted all legitimate options to render a more inclusive or humane decision. As for those who are marginalized by such a legal decision, they are entitled to a full, clear, and compassionate explanation of the decision. At that point, they will hopefully do their best to accept the decision and the system as a whole.

Second, there will always be some people who seem better situated or more privileged than others. There is always the possibility this can lead to resentment and quarreling. Perhaps the proper response is not covetousness, which is expressly prohibited by the Tenth Commandment. We can stop looking at the ways in which we feel we have been victimized. Instead, we perhaps can embrace the situations in which we find ourselves. Our situation may be out of our control, but our response is not, as the Talmud teaches, "Everything is in the hands of Heaven except for the fear of Heaven." Free choice applies to what actions we take, how we consider the consequences of our actions, and how we present ourselves as people, as Jews, and as representatives of the Torah. The Rabbis recognized that nobody receives everything they want:

Said R. Yudan in the name of R. Ibo: There is no man who leaves this world having achieved even half of his desires. If he has 100, he had wanted them to become 200; and if he had 200, he had wanted them to become 400 (*Kohelet Rabbah* 1:13).

The Great Principle of the Torah

Endnotes

1. The verse's feminine singular pronouns, *derakheha* (her ways) and *netivoteha* (her paths) are being interpreted by R. Joseph as referring to the Torah. However, "Torah" is not mentioned in those verses, and the feminine antecedents are *chokhmah* (wisdom) and *tevunah* (understanding). Nonetheless, *Metzudat David* says *chokhmah* and *tevunah* specifically refers to the Torah.

2. Hillel responded to a question from a potential convert; R. Akiva and Ben Azzai are quoted after Lev. 19:18 is included among the bases for exempting a person from a vow against another; the series of verses in *Bava Kamma* is presented in response to the *derashah* regarding the number 613 as the totality of commandments; and Bar Kappara's observation is the first of two comments that have nothing in common, other than they are both attributed to Bar Kappara.

3. R. Walter Wurzburger, "*Darkei Shalom*" (*Gesher: Bridging the Spectrum of Orthodox Jewish Scholarship*, Vol. 6, Student Organization of Yeshiva, 1977-8), p. 81.

4. R. Norman Lamm, in "Faith and Doubt" (see Chapter 1, endnote 2 for the bibliographical reference) discusses how belief vis-à-vis God could be defined either as "belief that"—a cognitive, factual awareness of the Divine, or "belief in"—an affective experience whereby an individual feels that he has a personal relationship with God. Nevertheless, it seems to me that when faith in God is discussed, the former type is assumed, unless otherwise indicated.

5. The syllogistic sequence of ideas would entail (1) God Himself "stands for" peace and pleasantness; (2) the Torah is given by God to man; and (3) the contents of the Torah definitively reflect peace and pleasantness, since these are intrinsic qualities of the Torah's Author and Giver. As a

consequence, God's intention is that a practitioner of the Torah should be more peaceful and personify pleasantness than were he not to observe the commandments. Furthermore, each mitzvah in its own right should be able to be perceived as an action that engenders peace and pleasantness.

6. In fact, only one person in the Tanakh is called *shalem*: "And Jacob came *shalem* to the city of Shechem, which is in the land of Canaan, when he came from Paddan-aram; and encamped before the city" (Gen. 33:18). Although most translations render this as "safely," the Talmud explains the verse differently, "Rav interpreted: Bodily whole, financially whole, and whole in his learning (*Shabbat* 33b, see also *Midrash Sechel Tov* 33:18). Jacob's "wholeness" was temporary, since he became profoundly fractured when Dinah was raped (Genesis 34) and Joseph sold (Genesis 37, see Rashi on Gen. 37:1).

7. See, e.g., *Gittin* 59a-b.

8. The Bar Ilan CD ROM search program lists 233 biblical references to *shalom*.

9. In *Otzar ha-Aggada me-ha-Mishnah ve-ha-Tosefta ha-Talmudim ve-ha-Midrashim ve-Sifrei ha-Zohar*, Vol. 3, Mosad ha-Rav Kook, Jerusalem, 5721, pp. 1268-73, "*shalom*" is cited in 173 different sources.

10. See *Shabbat* 23b.

11. See Mishnah *Pe'ah* 1:1.

12. Abraham: "And Abraham answered and said, 'Behold now, I have taken upon me to speak unto the Lord, who am but dust and ashes.'" (Gen. 18:27). Moses: "Now the man Moses was very humble, above all the men that were upon the face of the earth" (Num. 12:3).

13. According to Maimonides, this is not just for the scholar, but all people will benefit from contemplating God and recognizing one's own smallness (see *Yesodei ha-Torah* 2:2).

14. See Maimonides' commentary on the Mishnah, *Makkot* 3:16, cited in Chapter 3, for a different interpretation of this source.

15. "*Rav Yosef*" in *Entzyklopedia le-Chachmei ha-Talmud ve-ha-Gaonim*, Vol. 2, Yehoshua Orenstein, Yavneh, Tel Aviv, 1973, p. 551.

16. Places in the Talmud where R. Joseph uses biblical verses in order to resolve difficulties include: *Berakhot* 3b, 15b, 37b, 60a; *Pesachim* 68b, 86a; *Betzah* 5a; *Megillah* 16b; *Ketubot* 8b; *Kiddushin* 8a (2x), 76b; *Bava Metzia* 105a, 110b; *Bava Batra* 28b; *Sanhedrin* 16a, 19a, 61b; *Avodah Zarah* 24a, 24b; *Zevachim* 62a; and *Menachot* 22a.

17. *Entzyklopedia*, p. 552.

18. "Mishnah: When Rebbe [R. Yehudah ha-Nasi] died, humility and fear of sin ceased. Gemara: R. Joseph said to the Tanna: Do not include the word "humility," because there is I (*Sotah* 49b).

19. See *Kiddushin* 39a-b and *Sanhedrin* 61a-b.

20. See *Nedarim* 41a.

21. *Kiddushin* 31a.

22. In light of such an interpretation, it is interesting to note that Solomon's one request was not for pleasantness or peace, but for wisdom (1 Kings 3:5-9).

23. *The Psalms*, Jerusalem: Feldheim, 1978, pp. 194-5.

24. The Talmud teaches that the broken tablets were placed in the ark besides the whole ones (*Bava Batra* 14a-b).

25. See, e.g., Deut. 31:9.

26. The innermost part of the Temple. See 1 Kings 8:6.

27. See Exod. 25:20.

28. Avraham Even-Shoshan, *Konkordantziah Chadashah La-Torah, Nevi'im u-Ketuvim,* Jerusalem: Kiryat Sefer, 1965, pp. 1147-8.

29. Examples of statutory social limitation include: (a) a non-*kohen* is not accorded the privileges of a *kohen*; (b) a non-Levite is not accorded the privileges of a Levite; (c) a non-firstborn does not receive a double portion; (d) a king has certain privileges not accorded to civilians, and a king can only come from the tribe of Judah: (e) a woman does not have the same privileges as a man; (f) a *mamzer* is denied many marital privileges; (g) a *chalal* (a child from a *kohen* and a woman a *kohen* may not marry) loses the privileges of the priesthood; (h) Amalekites, male Moabites, Ammonites, and Egyptians have restrictions on converting to Judaism; (i) God commands the Jews to conquer the lands of the seven nations; (j) non-Jewish slaves are owned in perpetuity, and even their children are slaves; (k) deaf-mutes and the mentally challenged are not obligated to keep the commandments; (l) a woman whose husband is unwilling or unable to grant her a divorce cannot remarry in his lifetime; (m) if a wife of a *kohen* is raped, she cannot remain married to her husband. It is hard to imagine that many of these laws are compatible with the ideals of peace and pleasantness.

30. Blasphemy is forbidden by the Noahide code as well. The other six are murder, theft, idolatry, sexual immorality, eating the flesh of a living animal, and establishing courts (Tosefta, *Avodah Zarah* 9:4).

31. However, there is a famous rabbinic phrase that ranks merit above genealogy:

> A priest takes precedence over a Levite, a Levite over an Israelite, an Israelite over a *mamzer*.... This order of precedence applies only when all these were in other respects equal. If the *mamzer*

however was a scholar and the High Priest was an ignoramus, the learned *mamzer* takes precedence over the ignorant High Priest (*Horiyot* 13).

32. As of the date of publication, this story is available here, from which the English version has been translated: http://www.yeshiva.org.il/midrash/11847

Chapter 6

Lovingkindness

קהלת רבה (וילנא) פרשה ז

כתוב אחד אומר (שמואל א' כה:א) "וימת שמואל" וכתוב אחד אומר (שמואל א' כח:ג) "ושמואל מת." א"ר אסי "ושמואל מת" מיתה ודאי, "וימת שמואל" אין הדברים אמורים אלא לענין נבל שנא' (שמואל א' כ"ה) "וימת שמואל (וגו')" ואיש במעון." א"ר שמואל בר נחמן הכל סופדין וטופחין על מיתת הצדיק, וזה הרשע עושה לו מרזיחין, אמר ר' יהודה ללמדך שכל הכופר בגמילות חסד כאילו כופר בעיקר, אבל דוד המלך עליו השלום מה היה עושה? גומל חסד לכל! אומר כן "אפי' הורג או נהרג או רודף או נרדף, גומל אני לו חסד כמו לצדיק, הה"ד (תהלים י"ג) "ואני בחסדך בטחתי יגל לבי בישועתך אשירה לה' כי גמל עלי."

Kohelet Rabbah 7:4

One verse states, "And he died—Samuel [*u-Shmuel met*]…" (1 Sam. 25:1), and another states, "And Samuel died [*va-yamat Shmuel*]…" (1 Sam. 28:3).

Said R. Asi: "And Samuel died…" (28:3)—the actual death; "And he died—Samuel…" (25:1)—these words are said concerning Nabal, as it is said, "And he died—Samuel; and all Israel gathered themselves together, and

The Great Principle of the Torah

lamented him, and buried him in his house at Rama. And David arose, and went down to the wilderness of Paran. And there was a man [Nabal] in Maon, whose possessions were in Carmel; and the man was very great, and he had three thousand sheep, and a thousand goats; and he was shearing his sheep in Carmel" (1 Sam. 25:1-2) ["And Abigail came to Nabal; and, behold, he held a feast in his house, like the feast of a king; and Nabal's heart was merry within him, for he was very drunk; wherefore she told him nothing, less or more, until the morning light" (v. 36)].

Said R. Samuel bar Nachman: Everyone mourns and eulogizes as a result of the death of a righteous individual [like Samuel], and yet this evil doer [Nabal] makes for himself a party?

Said R. Yehudah: This is to teach you that anyone who denies [*kofer*][1] the centrality of acts of kindness,[2] it is as if he has denied the great principle of Judaism [*kofer be-ikkar*].[3]

But King David, peace be upon him, what did he do? He would engage in acts of kindness[4] for all. He would say the following: Whether the recently departed kills or is killed, pursues or is pursued, I will act towards the individual with kindness [I will eulogize him], as I would do for a truly righteous person. This is what is meant by the verse, "But as for me, in Your mercy do I trust; my heart shall rejoice in Your salvation. I will sing unto the Lord, because He has dealt bountifully with me" (Ps. 13:6).

Practical Applications of "Pleasantness" and "Peace"

In Chapter 5, we considered R. Joseph's opinion that the Torah is characterized by pleasantness and peace. However, a basic question can be raised to his formulation. It could be argued that R. Joseph's view does not demand overt actions or thoughts, but instead remains in the world of theory, not practice. A similar tension has already been identified between the final two views recorded in *Makkot* 24a of the prophets Amos and Habakkuk (Chapter 3) on the one hand, and Bar Kappara's position in *Berakhot* 63a (Chapter 4) on the other, i.e., how can essentially theoretical ideas be translated into practical daily realities. Perhaps R. Joseph's opinion is too theoretical. He seems to say that it is enough for an observant person to achieve a sense of overall personal peace through a life structured in accordance with Torah and *mitzvot*, especially if others judge the individual's actions as pleasant.

R. Yehudah in *Kohelet Rabbah* insists that according to the Torah, such sensibilities must be self-consciously translated into clear outward acts of kindness. Drawing on the example of Nabal, he goes so far as to say that failure to engage in deeds of kindness is not only inconsistent with Jewish values, but it is tantamount to denying the existence of God Himself![5] For R. Yehudah, promoting *gemilut chasadim* in such an extreme fashion not only indicates his basic understanding of Torah and *mitzvot*, but even his approach to the Jewish view of monotheism in general.

R. Yehudah's Source

R. Yehudah's statement is so extreme that it is worth seeking a textual source for his conclusion. R. Ze'ev Wolf Einhorn (the Maharzo, d. 1862), says R. Yehudah's opinion is based on the verse, "To the leader. Of David. The fool [*naval*] says in his heart, 'There is no God.' They are corrupt, they do abominable deeds; there is no one who does good" (Ps. 14:1). The simple reading of the verse is that the word *naval* means "fool," so the verse teaches that only foolish people deny the existence of God. Midrashically, however, R. Yehudah says David has singled out the biblical character Nabal as denying God, and David says further, "they [people like Nabal] do abominable deeds."

Learning from Nabal

The focus in the passage from *Kohelet Rabbah* 7 is Nabal, the first husband of Abigail, whom David eventually marries after Nabal's sudden demise.[6] The name "Nabal" means "abomination,"[7] leaving little to the imagination about how the Bible views his character.

In 1 Samuel 25, David comes to Nabal's estate, and David's men ask for provisions. Nabal responded, "Who is David? and who is the son of Jesse?" (1 Sam. 25:10). David becomes enraged, and prepares to take Nabal's estate by force, but Abigail pleads with David to not take such rash action, and David is finally calmed. As part of this process, Abigail says, "Let not my lord, I pray thee, regard this base fellow, even Nabal; for as his name is, so is he: Nabal is his name, and churlishness is with him; but I your handmaid saw not the young men of my lord, whom you did send" (1 Sam. 25:25). However, his specific infraction is an act of coldhearted ingratitude for the protection that David and his cohort had provided, rather than a failure to mourn the prophet Samuel.

Nabal's refusal to assist David and his men was reprehensible, but it might not have been illegal.[8] If it was not technically illegal, that might be what gave R. Yehudah room to criticize Nabal, not for his failure to sustain David in his time of need, but for failure to properly mourn for the prophet Samuel. Nabal's refusal to provide David's men with food was not even an instance of spiritual malfeasance, compared to his feasting during a time of national mourning. While David's men may have provided an important service to Nabal's shepherds, this protection had not been formally contracted, and therefore Nabal technically did not owe David anything.

Abigail, seeking to convince David that restraint was proper in this matter, insists to David that had she known of his request, she would have personally sent food, not because she had to, but out of gratitude and kindness. In verse 18, she actually does send provisions. Furthermore, she tells him that had David reacted violently to Nabal's refusal, it would have been viewed by all as an overreaction and would tarnish David's reputation (vv. 25-31).

Ignoring the simple meaning of this story about an unwillingness to share food with those who are hungry, the Midrash identifies a different action—Nabal's making a feast instead of mourning for the prophet Samuel (v. 36)—to indicate that he was self-absorbed, unkind, and insensitive to all that was going on around him. Equating Nabal's failure to mourn for Samuel with the sin of *kofer be-ikkar* leads one to conclude that acting unkindly undermines one's theological beliefs. According to R. Yehudah, such a person has missed the essential point of Judaism.

What Does Failure to Mourn Have to Do with *Chesed*?

In other statements, R. Yehudah indicated that a high standard of ethics and morality were more important to him than even his personal dignity and honor.

In one talmudic passage, R. Yehudah and R. Shimon are involved in making peace between husband and wife. R. Yehudah was prepared to humble himself, even though he was a great scholar, unlike R. Shimon, who refused to compromise his honor[9]:

> A man once said to his wife, "I vow that you benefit not from me, until you make R. Yehudah and R. Shimon taste of your cooking" [assuming they would never do so]. R. Yehudah tasted thereof, observing, "It is but logical: If, in order to make peace between husband and wife, the Torah commanded [as part of the *sotah* ritual], 'Let My name, written in sanctity, be dissolved in the utterances that curse, though her guilt is uncertain, how much more so [for me, when she is surely innocent]!"
>
> R. Shimon did not taste thereof, exclaiming, "Let all the widows' children perish," rather than that Shimon change his point of view, lest the Jewish people fall into the habit of vowing" (*Nedarim* 66b).

In another passage R. Yehudah is described as being prepared to sacrifice his Torah study, something extremely central to any rabbinic scholar, in order to carry out good deeds:

> Our Rabbis taught: One interrupts the study of the Torah for the sake of a funeral procession and escorting the bride. They tell of R. Yehudah b. Ila'i that he interrupted the study of the Torah for the sake of a funeral procession and escorting the bride (*Ketubot* 17a).

The Talmud often pits two value-laden activities against one another in an effort to draw conclusions regarding their respective importance.[10] Therefore R. Yehudah's preparedness to forego the honor of a Torah scholar, as well as even Torah study itself, in favor of showing kindness and concern for others, allows us to gain significant context regarding his striking statement in *Kohelet Rabbah* regarding the importance of mourning the death of a Torah personality, and by extension, all acts of interpersonal human kindness.

Using *Kohelet Rabbah* 7:4 to Understand Abraham
R. Yehudah's emphasis of the intrinsic connection between belief in God and acts of kindness calls to mind Abraham, in whom these two qualities went hand in hand. Historically, Abraham is viewed as the founding father of Judaism. He is described in rabbinic literature as discovering God in the midst of a society devoted to polytheism,[11] and promulgating his beliefs among whomever he came into contact. The acts of kindness which are associated specifically with Abraham—offering hospitality to strangers[12] as well as defending and rescuing those who are in danger[13]—could be pragmatically understood as constituting strategies by which Abraham could enhance his reputation[14] and thereby encourage converts to embrace his monotheistic beliefs. But taking the language of R. Yehudah literally, that one who does not engage in *chesed* is a *kofer be-ikkar*, leads to the conclusion that acts of kindness are not only means to an end of effecting religious commitment and devotion on the parts of others, but are clear manifestations of those beliefs by the practitioner himself.

Belief in the Jewish concept of God includes highlighting the following divine attributes, stated clearly in the Bible:

> The Lord passed before him [Moses], and proclaimed, 'The Lord, the Lord, a God merciful and gracious,

slow to anger, and abounding in steadfast love and faithfulness, keeping steadfast love for the thousandth generation, forgiving iniquity and transgression and sin… (Exodus 34:6-7).

Similarly, when Abraham was hosting, he emphasized that all compassion comes directly from God. Rashi writes, "After they would eat and drink, he would say to them, 'Bless the one who has given these things to you! Do you think that you have partaken from my food and drink? You have partaken from food of the One who brought the universe into existence!'" (Rashi on Gen. 21:33, s.v. *va-yikra sham*).

Belief in these divine attributes is combined with the conviction that man has been deliberately created in the image of God, as emphasized by Ben Azzai in Chapter 2. Therefore, underlying R. Yehudah's statement in *Kohelet Rabbah* is his perception that the biblical message can become manifest only when man acts in accordance with his innate Godliness. By doing so, man visibly demonstrates that mercy, grace, patience, goodness, and truth are to be found at his core, by virtue of his being in the image of God. One could then conclude that "*kofer be-ikkar*" not only relates to whether the individual believes in God, but also his understanding of his own essence. Nabal, by not acting kindly and in accordance with divine attributes, negated his own essence as having been created in the image God.

Walking in the Ways of God
In the book of Deuteronomy, man is repeatedly instructed to walk in the ways of God:

And you shall keep the commandments of the Lord your God, to walk in His ways and to fear Him (Deut. 8:6).

And now, Israel, what does the Lord your God require of you, but to fear the Lord your God, to walk in all His ways, and to love Him, and to serve the Lord your God with all your heart and with all your soul (Deut. 10:12).

For if you shall diligently keep this whole commandment[15] which I command you, to do it, to love the Lord your God, to walk in all His ways, and to cleave to Him (Deut. 11:22).

If you shall observe this entire commandment to do it, which I command you this day, to love the Lord your God, and to walk ever in His ways, then shall you add three cities [of refuge in Israel], beside these three [in Transjordan] (Deut. 19:9).

You have sworn to the Lord this day to be your God, and that you would walk in His ways, and keep His statutes and His commandments and His ordinances, and hearken to His voice (Deut. 26:17).

The Lord will establish you for a holy people unto Himself, as He has sworn to you; if you shall keep the commandments of the Lord your God, and walk in His ways (Deut. 28:9).

In that I command you this day to love the Lord your God, to walk in His ways, and to keep His commandments and

His statutes and His ordinances; then you shall live and multiply, and the Lord your God shall bless you in the land where you go in to possess it (Deut. 30:16).

A narrow reading of these verses would equate observing the commandments with walking in God's ways. Since God requires us to act in accordance with certain rules, compliance with these laws should be tantamount to walking in the ways that God has set before us. However, one could also understand that the phrase requires the Jewish people to go beyond the laws of the Torah and to emulate God's attributes even when not specifically enumerated as laws.[16]

A similar dichotomy is reflected in the interpretations offered by Nachmanides in Chapter 1 (pp. 25-26). First, Nachmanides argued that religious law serves as a starting point for more nuanced development of typical social contracts that societies formulate to maintain peace and stability. Second, Nachmanides also addressed the question of whether "doing the right and the good in the eyes of the Lord" is just another way of saying that one should observe the commandments, or indicates something else, a level beyond observance of the explicit commandments. It is altogether possible for an individual to comply with the commandments of the Torah without considering how these actions constitute either a declaration of God's existence, or taking into consideration God's plan for the universe in general and humanity in particular. This appears to be Nachmanides' concern elsewhere in his Torah commentary, where he develops the idea of *naval*[17] *bi-reshut ha-Torah,* someone who behaves boorishly though he never technically violates any *halakhah*:

"Speak unto all the congregation of the children of Israel, and say unto them: You shall be holy, for I the Lord your God am holy" (Lev. 19:2): And the matter is that the Torah warns against sexual transgressions (Leviticus 18) and prohibited foods (Lev. 17:10-16), but permits intimacy between husband and wife and the consumption of [kosher] meat and wine. Consequently a hedonist can find room to be unduly engaged in permitted sexual activity with his wife or multiple wives,[18] and could indulge in drunkenness and gluttony, and he could speak at will about all sorts of boorish matters [*neveilot*], since no explicit prohibitions against these activities are mentioned in the Torah, and he would be a boor within the confines of Torah law [*naval bi-reshut ha-Torah*].

Therefore the text comes, after delineating prohibitions that are completely prohibited, and commands regarding a type of general behavior—that we should separate ourselves from even those things that are permitted. One should limit his acts of intimacy... and should sanctify himself by consuming wine only in small measure.... And so he should separate himself from ritual impurity even though this is not explicitly stated in the Torah [except for *kohanim* and Nazirites].... And so he should guard his mouth and tongue from excessive eating and from disgusting speech.... And he should sanctify himself in this manner until he reaches the spiritual level of self-restraint [*perishut*].[19]

Regarding these things and similar activities comes this general commandment ["You shall be holy"], following the delineation of those transgressions that are completely prohibited, until the individual includes under this rubric the cleanliness of his hands and body.... The main thrust of this text warns that we should strive to be clean and pure and separate from the ways of human beings in general, who besmirch themselves with permitted indulgences and abominations (Nachmanides on Lev. 19:2).

Nachmanides, in addition to the negative activities and overindulgences to be avoided, also mentions the category of physical and spiritual cleanliness to be sought, all activities that could be categorized as *mitzvot bein adam le-atzmo* ("intrapersonal" commandments to help someone raise their own personal spiritual status). However, R. Yehudah appears to expand "You shall be holy" to include interpersonal commandments as well. He argues that unless the individual engages in acts of kindness, his connection with God is tenuous. For R. Yehudah, "walking in God's ways" goes beyond compliance with commandments and striving for personal purity; it requires a commitment to act in a Godly manner not only towards God and oneself, but towards everybody else as well.

In Chapter 3, we cited the seminal source in *Sotah* 14a describing some of these Godly attributes within the context of delineating the types of ethical activities that one should practice. R. Yehudah however attributes to acts of *chesed* a more central position, since their performance is a confirmation of actual belief in God.

There is a second talmudic source that readily supports R. Yehudah's distinction between strict *mitzvah*-observance and engaging in additional acts of kindness as a means to emulate God:

For it was taught: "This is my God and I will praise Him [*ve-anvehu*]" (Exod. 15:2): Adorn thyself before Him in the commandments. Make a beautiful *sukkah* in His honor, a beautiful *lulav*, a beautiful *shofar*, beautiful *tzitzit*, and a beautiful Torah scroll, and write it with fine ink, a fine reed, and a skilled scribe, and wrap it with beautiful silks. Abba Shaul interpreted, "And I will be like Him" [reading *ve-anvehu* as *ani ve-Hu*, "I and He"]: be like Him: just as He is gracious and compassionate, so you be gracious and compassionate (*Shabbat* 133b).

Abba Shaul could be understood to articulate a more personal manner in which the believer can demonstrate his admiration for the Divine. Not only should all of the things that one uses to worship God be exemplary and beautiful, but the worshipper himself should transform himself into a *cheftza shel mitzvah*—a beautiful object by which the commandments are practiced.

R. Yehudah might understand this approach differently. He might argue that Abba Shaul's insight acknowledges that God very much exists for the individual, and therefore the individual must actively model his own actions to make God's Presence manifest in the world. However, when an individual fails in this regard—or worse, deliberately avoids this charge—then, like Nabal, he is a *kofer be-ikkar*, failing to meet the requirements that belief in God demands, and such a person gives ample evidence that God is not a factor in how he lives his life.

Kindness and Jewish Identity
We have seen that according to R. Yehudah, if a person fails to engage in *chesed*, then that person's theological beliefs are to be

seriously doubted. A similar teaching relates that failure in this arena calls into questions one's identity as part of the Jewish people!

In the ninth chapter of the book of Joshua, the Gibeonites converted to Judaism under false pretenses, and as a result they were punished by being made into slaves. Later on, David decreed that the Gibeonites could never marry people who were born Jewish:

> As to the Netinim [Gibeonites], however, let them be summoned and we shall pacify them. Immediately the king called the Gibeonites, and said to them ... "What shall I do for you? And wherewith should I make atonement, that you may bless the inheritance of the Lord?" And the Gibeonites said to him, "Let seven men of his [Saul's] sons be delivered unto us and we will hang them up unto the Lord..." (2 Sam. 21:6). He tried to pacify them, but they would not be pacified. Thereupon he said to them: "This nation [Israel] is distinguished by three characteristics: They are merciful, modest, and benevolent [*rachmanim, baishanim ve-gomlei chasadim*].... Only one who cultivates these three characteristics is fit to join this nation" (*Yevamot* 79a).

This source suggests that the values of the members of God's people must be ultimately consonant with God's own values. Yet all people fall short of the level of perfection associated with God. How then can any group be God's people? The answer is that this passage does not require perfection, but fulfillment of these three qualities: mercy, humility, and loving-kindness. Despite man's inherent imperfections, this passage in *Yevamot* teaches that when an entire nation like the Gibeonites calls for cruelty without being pacified, such a people must be condemned for the unrelenting cruelty they endorse.

It is not just a philosophical ideal to say that the Jewish people is personified by its commitment to acts of kindness, as Maimonides codifies this teaching as a matter of Jewish law:

> We operate under the presumption that all [Jewish] families are of acceptable lineage and it is permitted to marry their descendants as an initial and preferred option. Nevertheless, if you see two families continuously quarreling with each other, or you see one family that is always involved with strife and controversy, or you see a person who frequently quarrels with people in general and is very insolent, we suspect [their lineage as not being Jewish]. It is proper to distance oneself from such people for these are disqualifying characteristics. Similarly, a person who always slurs the lineage of others, casting aspersions on the lineage of families or individuals, claiming that they are *mamzerim*, we are suspicious that he himself is a *mamzer*. Similarly, if he calls others slaves, we suspect that he is a slave. For whoever disparages others, disparages them with a blemish that he himself possesses. Similarly, whenever a person is characterized by insolence and cruelty, hating people and not showing kindness to them, we seriously suspect that he is a Gibeonite. For the distinguishing signs of the holy nation of Israel is that they are modest, merciful, and benevolent.[20] With regard to the Gibeonites, "The Gibeonites are not of the Jewish people" (2 Sam. 21:2). For

they acted extremely brazenly and would not be appeased. They did not show mercy to the sons of Saul, nor did they show kindness to the Jews to forgive the descendants of their king, while [the Jews] had shown them kindness and allowed them to live (*Issurei Bi'ah* 19:17).

It is true that stereotyping against any nation, even the Gibeonites, may create problems, because we cannot be certain that every member of a group has the same character defects. However, Maimonides, in another passage, repeats a broad characterization of the difference between Jews and others:

> A person will never become impoverished from giving charity. No harm nor damage will ever be caused because of charity, as it says, "And the deed of charity is peace" (Isa. 32:17). Everyone who is merciful evokes mercy from others, as it says, "And He shall grant you mercy and shower mercy upon you and multiply you" (Deut. 13:18). Whenever a person is cruel and does not show mercy, his lineage is suspect, for cruelty is found only among the gentiles, as it says, "They are cruel and will not show mercy" (Jer. 50:42). The entire Jewish people and all those who attach themselves to them are as brothers, as it says, "You are children unto God your Lord" (Deut. 14:1). And if a brother will not show mercy to a brother, who will show mercy to him? To whom do the poor of Israel lift up their eyes? To the gentiles who hate them and pursue them? Behold their eyes are pointed to their brethren alone (*Matnot Ani'im* 10:2).

While Maimonides' animosity towards non-Jews is evident from this source, the expectations for the interrelationships among the Jewish people are equally unambiguous.

Assisting People Who Have Poor Character

It is important to note that despite Maimonides' apparent negative attitude towards the charitableness of non-Jews, he nevertheless codifies how it is a *mitzvah* for Jews to support the non-Jewish poor:

> Our Sages commanded us to visit the gentiles when ill, to bury their dead in addition to the Jewish dead, and support their poor in addition to the Jewish poor for the sake of peace. Behold, it says, "God is good to all and His mercies extend over all His works" (Ps. 145:9), and it says, "Her ways are ways of pleasantness and all its paths are peace" (Prov. 3:17) (*Melakhim* 10:12).

It is true that the phrase "for the sake of peace" could be understood in utilitarian terms; perhaps only when peace between peoples is endangered do these things need to be done, and when no threat is perceived, there is no responsibility towards non-Jews. However, R. Walter Wurzberger contends that since Maimonides added the verse, "God is good to all and His mercies extend over all His works," he believed that "walking in God's ways" means to be kind to all of His creatures, regardless of their religion.

R. Yedudah's Emphasis on *Gemilut Chasadim*

In the end, it would appear that R. Yehudah in *Kohelet Rabbah* goes much further than either the passage in *Yevamot* or Maimonides in defining the essential Jewish trait. Whereas Maimonides merely excludes individuals or families that are cruel and contentious, R. Yehudah posits that not only must bad acts and attitudes be eradicated, but there should also be positive traits that can be readily identified. Just because someone is not cruel does not mean they constantly engage in acts of *chesed*. It is fair to realize that if someone were to spend all of one's hours engaged in acts of kindness, there would be no time remaining for study, working, or building a family. Nevertheless, in order to meet R. Yehudah's criteria, acts of kindness would have to be regular and everyday occurrences, rather than occasional or rare events.

Implications for Contemporary Jews
R. Yehudah's insistence that an observant Jew engage regularly in acts of kindness, not as a manifestation of good character traits, but as a fundamental part of his religious activity and a reflection of his conception of God, constitutes, in my opinion, a radical departure from how many observant Jews understand their responsibilities towards their fellow man. Of course, some Jews devote themselves to Jewish communal service, so their work-lives are defined by helping, instructing, and advising others. And when these individuals engage in such activities *lishmah*—for their own sake, rather than for an ulterior motive—they significantly and meaningfully blur the natural dichotomy between one's religious and professional lives. However, it seems to me that most Jews consider *gemilut chasadim* as an optional enterprise, that while admirable, is nevertheless not mandated to the same extent as prayer, Shabbat, and *kashrut*.

In the Ten Commandments, God says, "I am the Lord your God, who brought you out of the land of Egypt, out of the house of bondage" (Exod. 20:2, Deut. 5:6). Just as God identifies Himself in one of the most central verses of the Torah as a Redeemer and Helper of those in need, so too should all who are in God's image strive to do the same. Yet some Jews are oblivious to the implications of this verse of the Ten Commandments, even to the point of not viewing this verse as a *mitzvah*, but as a theoretical postulate upon which all other Commandments are premised.[21]

One often hears how individual Jewish communities are rated by how warm or kindhearted they are. R. Yehudah projects an ideal where all Jewish communities and the individuals who comprise them by definition would constantly display qualities and acts that universally reflect an ethic of sensitivity and consideration to one and all.

There is a rabbinic concept of *kove'a ittim la-Torah*, setting aside times every day for Torah study.[22] One could argue that there should similarly be a concept of *kove'a ittim le-gemilut chasadim*. This would allow for individual differences regarding time available, inclination, and opportunities, but still promote a proactive approach to assuring a person's direct engagement in *chesed* initiatives.

As to what is taught in synagogues and day schools, R. Yehudah's perspective would require that whenever theological matters are being presented, it is necessary to reinforce how issues of belief should directly lead to study and contemplation; how theoretical matters of God's immanence and transcendence can be translated into practical terms in different forms of *gemilut chasadim*.

A final theoretical implication of R. Yehudah's view is to reject the dichotomy between *mitzvot bein adam la-Makom* and *mitzvot bein adam le-chavero*. Such a distinction should be rejected as artificial, as R. Yehudah would maintain that it is impossible to properly believe in God and not frequently engage in acts of *chesed*, since those are the true manifestations of God's attributes.

Endnotes

1. The previous formulations were all in the positive: Hillel said "This is the entire Torah" (Chapter 1); "This is the major principle [*kelal gadol*]" (Chapter 2); "This is a greater principle" (Chapter 2); "There came David and reduced them to eleven…" (Chapter 3); "A short text upon which all of the essential principles of the Torah depend" (Chapter 4); "The entire Torah is because of…" (Chapter 5). However, the switch from affirmative to negative does not need to bother us, because a converse of a positive also serves to place emphasis on a particular issue. When someone states that failure to engage in lovingkindness is tantamount to negating the entire Torah, he means that this omission negates whatever other good the individual may have achieved.

2. All kindnesses extended to the dead, including preparing the individual for burial, accompanying the individual to his final resting place, digging the grave, and delivering a eulogy, are categorized as *chesed shel emet*, "true acts of kindness," since it can hardly be expected that the individual will reciprocate what has been done on his behalf.

3. This phrase is usually used in reference to someone who denies God entirely (*Sanhedrin* 38b, 45b), so it is striking that this rabbinic statement uses *kofer be-ikkar* not about God's existence, but about the importance of kindness.

4. Although the term *gemilut chasadim* includes a number of different acts of kindness extended to others, the Midrash singles out eulogies as a singular example of it. In the Bible, David delivered several eulogies: for David and Jonathan (2 Sam. 1:17-27), and his son Absalom (2 Sam. 19:1-5).

5. Rabbinic tradition equates certain negative activities with denying God's existence:

> R. Yochanan said in the name of R. Shimon b. Yochai: Every man in whom is haughtiness of spirit… R. Yochanan himself said: He is as though he had denied the fundamental principle; as it is said: "Your heart be arrogant and you forget the Lord your God…" (Deut. 8:14) (*Sotah* 4b).
>
> And R. Yochanan said in the name of R. Joseph b. Zimra: One who bears evil tales almost denies the foundation [of faith], as it is said: "Who have said: Our tongue will we make mighty; our lips are with us; who is Lord over us?" (Ps. 12:5) (*Arakhin* 15b).
>
> The evil son, what does he say? "What is this service to you?" (Exod. 12:26) — "to you," and not to him. And because he excluded himself from the totality [of the Jewish people] and denied the fundamental principle, you shall set his teeth on edge and say to him, "For the sake of this did God do for me when I left Egypt" (Exod. 13:8)—for me and not for you. Had you been there, you would not have been redeemed (*Mekhilta de-R. Shimon bar Yochai, Parashat Bo, Masekhta de-Pischa* 18).

However, failure to perform acts of *chesed* is a sin of omission rather than commission, and suggests that such activities are assumed to be positive prerequisites of Judaism, rather than negative indications of rebellion and disdain.

6. See 1 Sam. 25:37-42.

7. See Francis Brown, S.R. Driver, and Charles A. Briggs, *A Hebrew and English Lexicon of the Old Testament*, Oxford (England), Clarendon Press, p. 614. It is difficult to imagine that someone would name their child "Nabal," i.e., "abomination." Yehudah Kil, in *Da'at Mikra* on 1 Sam. 25:2 suggests among other interpretations, that the name originally may have been associated with *neiveil*, a musical instrument similar to a harp, or an earthenware jug, as in ibid. 1:24.

8. R. Moshe Isserles (the Rema, 1520-1572) writes:

> Every person on whose behalf another person performs an action or does a favor, cannot say, "You did this without expectation of compensation because I did not ask you," but he must pay him in accordance with what he has done (*Choshen Mishpat* 264:4).

These words, based on the Ran, indicate that Nabal would have been obligated to compensate David for the protection he provided. However, Rabbi Hayyim ben Avraham Algazi clarifies:

> This is only if he improved his [the other's] property, e.g., he said to him, "eat with me" or "live with me," then one is obligated to pay for what has been done.... However if he has only saved the other from suffering some kind of damage, then he is to be treated as one who has "caused an attacking lion to flee" or one who has returned a lost object [he is compensated for expenses but nothing more] (*Netivot ha-Mishpat* 7).

If David and his men actually saved Nabal's property, then according to the Rema, Nabal would not only have had to be nice to them and offer them food, but he would have to pay them their expenses. However, it is unclear from the biblical account whether such conditions were met. Therefore, at best, giving food to David and his men would be an act of *chesed*, which Nabal was not interested in doing.

9. In some matters, a scholar is allowed to waive his requisite honor. See, e.g., *Kiddishin* 32a-b.

10. This is essentially a basic technique of "Values Clarification," an educational program for teaching moral development based upon the work of the moral psychologist Lawrence Kohlberg developed in the 1970's and 80's. Dilemmas are created where absolute choices have to be

made, thereby indicating priorities and preferences in various situations. This is common in talmudic discourse; see, e.g., *Megillah* 3a-b, which discusses the relative values of Temple service, hearing the Megillah on Purim, and burying a *met mitzvah*.

11. See, e.g., Maimonides, *Hilkhot Avodah Zarah* 1:3.

12. See Gen. 18:1-8.

13. Gen. 14:13-6, 17:15-20, 18:23ff.

14. See Gen. 12:2, 8; 13:3-4, 8; Gen. 14:19-22; Gen. 17:4-5, 18-20; Gen. 18:18-19; 21:22-23; 23:5-6; 24:48-50.

15. The use of the singular word *mitzvah*, "commandment" (Deut. 11:22; 19:9) as opposed to the more common *mitzvot*, "commandments" (Deut. 8:6; 26:17; 28:9 and 30:16) supports the rabbinic view that on a certain level, all of the Torah's commandments share a basic, common denominator—to carry out the will of God. Consequently, they can all be viewed as distinct forms of a single imperative.

16. Each one of these verses could be read in both manners: either "walking in God's ways" means keeping the commandments, or it means emulating the divine attributes, even beyond the technical commandments. Each time the phrase "walk in His ways" is used, it can restrict and refine what the previous phrase means ("to keep the commandments"), or it means something additional, above and beyond the commandments, and to emulate God's ways in all cases.

17. The word *naval* in this context should be understood in the generic sense rather than as a direct reference to the biblical character in 1 Samuel 25. Nevertheless, the association between the biblical character and the common noun underscores the point.

18. Ashkenazim prohibited polygamy in the year 1000 with the decree of Rabbenu Gershom ben Yehudah, and most Sephardim have shunned the practice as well.

19. Although an absolute definition of *perishut* would suggest that an individual must separate himself from any and all forms of sensuous activity, Nachmanides is promoting a more nuanced approach. While the individual should not overindulge in such behaviors, Nachmanides also does not see celibacy and fasting as ultimate values either. For Nachmanides, holiness is about disciplined moderation rather than self-denial.

20. Maimonides quotes these qualities in a different order. Where the Talmud has *rachmanim, baishanim, ve-gomlei chasadim*, Maimonides inverts the order of the first two: *baishanim, rachmanim, ve-gomlei chasadim*.

21. See the essay by R. Moshe Tzuriel, entitled, "Is 'Anochi' One of the 613 Commandments or Not?" available as of the publication of this book at http://www.yeshiva.org.il/midrash/5582 in which he discusses the positions of the *Baal Halakhot Gedolot*, among others, based upon a passage in the *Mekhilta*, that the first statement in the Ten Commandments is not to be counted as a *mitzvah* by itself.

22. See Maimonides, *Talmud Torah* 1:8.

Chapter 7

Lawfulness

שמות רבה (וילנא) פרשת משפטים פרשה ל יט
א"ר אלעזר: כל התורה תלויה במשפט, לכך נתן הקדוש ברוך הוא דיניו אחר עשרת הדברות. לפי שהבריות מעבירין על הדין והוא נפרע מהם ומלמד את באי עולם, שלא הפך את סדום עד שעברה את הדין שנאמר (יחזקאל טז) "גאון שבעת לחם ושלות השקט", ואף ירושלים לא גלתה עד שעברה את הדין, שנאמר (ישעיה א) "יתום לא ישפוטו וריב אלמנה לא יבא אליהם", ולמה נתן הקדוש ברוך הוא כתר ליהודה? — והלא לא לבדו הוא גבור מכל אחיו, והלא שמעון ולוי גבורים והאחרים, אלא שדן דין אמת לתמר, לכן נעשה דיין העולם, משל לדיין שבא דין של יתומה לפניו וזיכה אותה, כך יהודה בא דין תמר לפניו שתשרף, והוא זיכה אותה מפני שמצא לה זכות, כיצד היו יצחק ויעקב יושבים שם וכל אחיו והיו מחפין אותו, הכיר יהודה למקום ואמר אמיתת הדבר ואמר (בראשית לח) "צדקה ממני" ועשאו הקדוש ברוך הוא נשיא, וכן היה בן זומא אומר ודורש נתביישת בעולם הזה אין אתה מתבייש מן הקדוש ברוך הוא לעולם הבא שהוא אש אוכלה, למה שאין בושתו של העולם הזה כלום אלא בושת עמידתו של העולם הבא, שנאמר (תהלים לב) "על זאת יתפלל כל חסיד אליך וגו'".

Exodus Rabbah 30:19

Said R. Elazar: The entire Torah is based on justice [*mishpat*]. Therefore the Holy One, blessed be He, gave the civil law code immediately after the Ten Commandments.[1] This is because people transgress the law and He punishes them and thereby teaches all of humanity [to act with justice].[2] Sodom was not destroyed until they transgressed this type of law, as it says, "Behold, this was the iniquity of your sister Sodom: pride, fullness of bread, and careless ease was in her and in her daughters; neither did she strengthen the hand of the poor and needy" (Ezek. 16:49).

And also Jerusalem, its inhabitants were not exiled until they had transgressed civil law, as it is written, "Your princes are rebellious, and companions of thieves; every one loves bribes, and follows after rewards; they judge not the fatherless, neither does the cause of the widow come to them." (Isa. 1:23).

And why did the Holy One, blessed be He, give kingship to Judah?[3] Surely he was not the only mighty one among Jacob's children, but Shimon and Levi as well as others! Rather because he judged properly regarding Tamar, and for this reason he was designated the judge for eternity. It is a parable of a judge before whom came the case of an orphan, and he vindicated her. So too the case of Tamar who came before Judah accused of a crime punishable by execution, and he vindicated her because he found a merit on her behalf.[4] How was it? Isaac and Jacob were sitting there along with his brothers and they defended him. Judah recognized the claim and rendered the correct verdict, and he said, "She is more righteous than I" (Gen. 38:26), and the Holy One, blessed be He, declared him to be a prince. And so Ben Zoma used to say, "You were humiliated in this world. You will not be humiliated before the Holy One, blessed be He, in the World to Come, because He is a consuming fire." Because humiliation in this world is insignificant [compared to] humiliation arising from one's standing in the World to Come, as it is said, "For this let everyone that is faithful pray unto You in a time when You may be found; surely, when the great waters overflow, they will not reach unto him" (Ps. 32:6).

Is Justice a Religious or Secular Value?
Chapters 1 and 2 explored the opinions of Hillel, R. Akiva, and Ben Azzai, and how the highest values are different forms of interpersonal behavior. Chapter 3 was devoted to discerning the essential point of Judaism, based on a group of twenty-four biblical phrases. Chapter 4 explained Bar Kappara's opinion that belief in and knowledge of God formed the frame of reference for living a spiritual, meaningful life. In Chapter 5, we considered R. Joseph's conclusion that the Torah should be defined by the values of pleasantness and peace. Chapter 6 addressed R. Yehudah's view that failure to engage in acts of kindness calls into question one's faith and religiosity. However, R. Elazar's focus in *Exodus Rabbah* 30 is that legal justice lies at the heart of the Torah. This opinion appears to address a very different aspect of society. It would appear that justice is a civil function of society, not a religious one, so it is strange that R. Elazar would raise a secular value to the highest position in a religious framework.

As we have pointed out in Chapter 1, Maimonides insists that, due to the diversity of human beings, if there were no laws governing human relationships, weaker people would be victimized by the stronger. Therefore, to prevent such abuses, systems of law, both religious and secular, are needed to govern society. Consequently, it is not enough that religious life results in some positive actions and attitudes. If religious people are thought to be criminal and corrupt, or worse, the thought develops that these evil traits are inherent in religion itself, nobody would ever believe such a religious system has any value at all.

Perhaps it should be said that justice is not only a religious value, but also a prerequisite in order that the religion can positively influence its practitioners as well as society in general. Disrespect for the law—both Jewish and secular—by religious individuals is a major factor in the perpetuation of *Chillul Hashem* (profaning the name of God), one of the most profoundly reprehensible of all sins.[5] And for those looking at Judaism from without, such hypocrisy could be a central reason for rejecting out-of-hand such a lifestyle. We have pointed out in Chapter 5 that there are some who will feel victimized by even proper applications of the law. But when religious principles are intentionally applied unfairly and unevenly, it is obvious that the outside world will view religion and its followers with disdain.[6]

R. Elazar's Motivation

Rabbi Akiva, who championed, "And you shall love your neighbor as yourself," had five main students: R. Meir, R. Yehudah, R. Yosi, R. Shimon, and R. Elazar b. Shammua, and the Talmud says, "it was they who revived Torah at that time" (*Yevamot* 62b). Rashi, in his commentary on the Talmud, states that wherever a person named "R. Elazar" is mentioned in the Mishnah or a Baraita, it is referring to R. Elazar b. Shammua (Rashi on *Shabbat* 19b, s.v., *Rabbi Elazar hu*). This R. Elazar was also among the last individuals to receive true *semikhah* (rabbinic ordination)[7] during the Roman persecutions:

> Once the wicked government decreed that whoever conferred ordination should be put to death, and whoever received ordination should he put to death, the city in which the ordination took place demolished, and the boundaries wherein it had been conferred, uprooted. What did R. Yehudah b. Bava do? He went and sat between two great mountains between two large cities; between the Shabbat boundaries of the cities of Usha and Shefaram, and there ordained five elders: R. Meir, R. Yehudah, R. Shimon, R. Yosi, and R. Elazar ben Shammua.... As soon as their enemies discovered them. He [R. Yehudah b. Bava] urged them, "My children, flee." They said to him, "What will become of you, Rabbi?" "I will lie before them like a stone which none [can] overturn," he replied. It was said that the enemy did not stir from the spot until they had driven three hundred iron spear-heads into his body, making it like a sieve (*Sanhedrin* 14a).

Consequently, R. Elazar was an eye-witness to the destruction of Jerusalem and the persecutions that the Jews suffered at the hands of the Romans. The land of Israel was very beloved to R. Elazar, as indicated by the following Midrash:

> A story concerning R. Elazar ben Shammua and R. Yochanan ha-Sandlar who were walking to Netzivim [a

town in Babylonia], to the yeshiva of R. Yehudah ben Beteira to learn Torah from him: They reached Tzidon and remembered the land of Israel. Their eyes filled, and tears flowed, and they tore their garments and recited the following verse: "When the Lord your God shall cut off the nations from before you, where you go in to dispossess them, and you dispossess them, and dwell in their land" (Deut. 12:29). They then turned around and went back to their original place. They said, "Dwelling in the land of Israel is equivalent to all of the commandments of the Torah" (*Sifrei, Parashat Re'eh* 80).

Based on this story, one could imagine that R. Elazar repeatedly tried to make sense of what had befallen his people. We can imagine that he asked himself what caused the destruction of the Temple, as well as the loss of political sovereignty and religious freedom.

R. Joseph B. Soloveitchik has written in *Kol Dodi Dofek* that it is essentially frustrating and futile for man to speculate why terrible things happen. Our primary concern in the aftermath of a terrible event, he states, is to determine the proper response:

> ... Evil exists, and I will neither deny it or camouflage it with vain intellectual gymnastics. I am concerned about evil from a halakhic standpoint, like a person who wishes to know the deed which he shall do; I ask one simple question: What must the sufferer do so that he may live through his suffering? ... We do not inquire about the hidden ways of the Almighty, but, rather, the path wherein man shall walk when suffering strikes.... How shall a person act in a time of trouble?[8]

Consequently, if R. Elazar was only reflecting on why these terrible events occurred, he could be criticized, since the answer is impossible to find. However if he was thinking how to properly respond, and how to improve society in the face of these tragedies, then his thought process is entirely valid, based on this passage from Rabbi Soloveitchik. Personal reflection is constructive when it leads to future actions that are beneficial to society.

The prophet Isaiah simultaneously criticized Jerusalem and the sister territory Judah for their shortcomings, while also, by implication, offering a prescription for improvement:

> How is the faithful city become a harlot! She that was full of justice, and righteousness lodged within her, but now murderers [are found instead]. Your silver is become dross, your wine mixed with water. Your princes are rebellious, and companions of thieves; everyone loves bribes, and follows after rewards; they judge not the fatherless, neither does the cause of the widow come to them (Isa. 1:21-23).

R. Elazar cited v. 23 as his source that justice is the highest value in Judaism. Whereas verses 16-17 criticize the deplorable state of the society, vv. 21-23 serve as guides for the restoration of the city to its former glory. Isaiah condemns Israel for being unjust, harboring murderers, devaluing precious metals, diluting wine, and failing to defend the widow and orphan. Implicit in Isaiah's words is that these actions must be reversed.

The underlying assumption of Isaiah's passage is the principle of *middah ke-neged middah*, the divine principle of "measure for measure." Therefore in the case of Jerusalem, Isaiah contends that since the affairs of the city were not conducted fairly and compassionately, the infrastructure that enabled such treatment obviously must be destroyed.

However, there are other opinions about what caused the destruction of Jerusalem; R. Elazar does not have the only opinion about why Jerusalem was destroyed. In light of these numerous explanations, R. Elazar would then have to be understood as arguing that the most obvious rationale for the destruction of the Temples was the failure of Jerusalem to institute and maintain just practices.

In Noah's time, only a few generations after the Creation, the world was filled with *chamas* (Gen. 6:11), a broad word that encompasses violence, injustice, and other types of corruption.[9] In response, God decided to destroy His creation by means of a flood and start again. Jerusalem was supposed to exemplify the best practices which organized humanity could achieve,[10] so its continued existence could not be justified if it didn't fulfill this purpose. When divine expectations are high, the consequences of non-compliance can be extensive and dramatic.[11]

R. Elazar perhaps entertained the same view articulated by Isaiah, when the prophet states very clearly, "Zion shall be redeemed with justice [*mishpat*], and they that return of her with righteousness [*tzedakah*]" (Isa. 1:27). The inverse is that a lack of justice and righteousness will not lead to the redemption of Jerusalem, but its destruction.

R. Elazar's Three Arguments

R. Elazar presents three arguments for his opinion that the central principle of the Torah is "justice." First, he begins with a textual proof: the civil laws (*mishpatim*) immediately follow the Ten Commandments, and by implication that is a place of prominence in the Torah. In textual interpretation, this method is called *semikhut ha-parashiyot*, the juxtaposition of two biblical passages to demonstrate a relationship or common theme.

The second argument is that two major cities in the land of Israel, Sodom and Jerusalem, were both destroyed because they did not pursue justice in their daily activities. Sodom was a non-Jewish city, whereas Jerusalem was not only a Jewish city, but the heart of Jewish religious and cultural life. According to R. Elazar, the common denominator that led to the destruction of these two metropolises was an absence of justice.

His third argument is drawn from the personal example of the biblical figure Judah, progenitor of the kings of the house of David. R. Elazar maintains that it was Judah's singular act of justice regarding his daughter-in-law Tamar that earned him his position as ancestor to the eternal Jewish kingship.

R. Elazar's First Argument: Juxtaposition of Biblical Themes
The principle of *semikhut ha-parashiyot* (juxtaposition of biblical passages) is used in several contexts. Sometimes it is used to create a legal imperative or ideal. In other cases, it can teach an ethical or exegetical lesson, even if it is not codified in a specific halakhic mandate. For example, in our discussion of Nabal, we saw that two events were written in proximity: the death of the prophet Samuel, and Nabal's boorishness, including a lavish feast that he hosted. This led R. Yehudah to conclude that Nabal made a feast for himself while the rest of the nation was in mourning.

R. Elazar uses this hermeneutical principle in a similar way. On some level, the Ten Commandments are the cornerstone of Jewish law, but they are too vague to have a practical application. As a result, the societal laws that follow, the *mishpatim*, are given a place of prominence. Even if someone would disagree with R. Elazar's conclusion that justice is the highest value in Judaism, nonetheless all the laws that pertain to justice and righteousness would remain equally binding.

Furthermore, we can return to Nachmanides' teaching that the Torah did not dictate the proper response to every situation in life. Hence the Torah gave certain general principles as guides, when a specific situation did not have an absolute answer. R. Elazar might say, similar to Nachmanides, that familiarity with the value of *mishpat* will instruct us on how to live our lives in all those cases where no specific *halakhah* seems to apply. Furthermore, if someone is about to embark on an illegal, immoral, or improper endeavor, perhaps if that person realizes that justice is a central value of Judaism, they will take pause before following through on that plan.[12]

R. Elazar's Second Argument:
No Justice in Sodom or Jerusalem

R. Elazar's second argument is based on how the Bible itself explains the sins of Sodom and Gomorrah, and later on how the sins of Jerusalem are described.

In both the Bible as well as in rabbinic literature, Sodom and Gomorrah are held up as quintessential dens of iniquity. In the Torah, there are very few sins that are attributed to the Sodomites, with the one glaring exception being their demands to rape Lot's guests (Gen. 19:4-11). However, the Rabbis are quite expansive about Sodom's transgressions, listing approximately twenty infractions when it comes to describing both general and specific practices reflecting the overall lack of justice in these cities:

Now the men of Sodom were wicked and sinners against the Lord exceedingly (Gen. 13:13).

And the Lord said: "Verily, the cry of Sodom and Gomorrah is great, and, verily, their sin is exceedingly grievous" (Gen. 18:20).

But before they lay down, the men of the city, even the men of Sodom, surrounded the house, both young and old, all the people from every quarter. And they called to Lot, and said to him, "Where are the men that came to you this night? Bring them out unto us, that we may know them." And Lot went out to them to the door, and shut the door after him. And he said, "Please, my brothers, do not act so wickedly. Behold now, I have two daughters that have not known man; let me, please, bring them out to you, and do to them as is good in your eyes; only to these men do nothing; because they have come under the shadow of my roof." And they said, "Stand back." And they said, "This one fellow came to sojourn, and he wishes to play the judge; now will we deal worse with you, than with them." And they pressed upon the man Lot, and drew near to break down the door. But the men put forth their hand, and brought Lot into the house to them, and the door they shut. And they smote the men that were at the door of the house with blindness, both small and great; so that they wearied themselves to find the door (Gen. 19:4-11).

Then the Lord caused to rain upon Sodom and Gomorrah brimstone and fire from the Lord out of Heaven (v. 24).

Lawfulness

The following long talmudic passage ascribes over twenty sins to the people of Sodom and Gomorrah:

> Our Rabbis taught: The men of Sodom have no portion in the future world, as it is written, "But the men of Sodom were wicked and sinners before the Lord exceedingly": "wicked" — in this world, "and sinners" — in the world to come.
>
> Rav Yehudah said: "Wicked" — (1) with their bodies [i.e., sexual immorality]; "and sinners" — (2) with their money; "before the Lord" refers to (3) blasphemy; "exceedingly" — (4) they intentionally sinned....
>
> Our Rabbis taught: The men of Sodom waxed haughty only on account of the good which the Holy One, blessed be He, had lavished upon them....
>
> They said: Since there comes forth bread from the earth, and it has the dust of gold, why should we tolerate wayfarers, who come to us only to deplete our wealth? Come, let us (5) abolish the practice of travelling in our land....
>
> Rava gave the following exposition: What is meant by the verse, "How long will you imagine mischief against a man? You shall be slain all of you: you are all as a bowing wall, and as a tottering fence" (Ps. 62:4)? This teaches that they used (6) to cast [envious] eyes at wealthy men, place them by a leaning wall, thrust it upon them, then go and take their wealth."
>
> Rava expounded: What is meant by the verse, "In the dark they dig through houses, which they had marked for themselves in the daytime: they know not the light" (Job

24:16)? This teaches that they used (6a) to cast [envious] eyes at wealthy men, and entrust balsam into their keeping, which they [the wealthy men] placed in their storerooms. In the evening they would come and smell it out like dogs.... Then they would go, burrow in, and steal the money, [and as for their victim] (6b) they cause him to go naked without clothing....

They (7) lead away the donkey of the fatherless; they (8) take the widow's ox for a pledge; they (9) remove the landmarks; they (10) violently take away flocks, and feed them. And he [the victim] shall be (10a) brought to the grave, and shall remain in the tomb.... They ruled: (11) He who has [only] one ox must tend [all the oxen of the town] for one day; but he who has none must tend [them] two days. Now a certain orphan, the son of a widow, was given oxen to tend. He went and killed them and said to them [the Sodomites], "He who has an ox, let him take one hide; he who has none, let him take two hides." "What is the meaning of this?" they exclaimed. Said he, "The final usage [i.e., the disposal of the ox when dead] must be as the initial one; just as the initial usage is that he who possesses one ox must tend for one day, and he who has none must tend two days; so should be the final usage: he who has one ox should take one hide, and he who has none should take two."

[Likewise, they ruled] (12) He who crosses with the ferry must pay one *zuz*, but he who does not, [entering by another way] must give two. (13) If one had rows of bricks every person came and took one, saying, "I have taken only one." (13a) If one spread out garlic or onions [to dry them], every person came and took one, saying, "I have taken only one."

There were four judges in Sodom, [named] Shakrai, Shakurai, Zayyafi, and Mazle Dina.

Now, (14) if a man assaulted his neighbor's wife and bruised her, they would say [to the husband]: "Give her to him, that she may become pregnant for you." (15) If one cut off the ear of his neighbor's ass, they would order, "Give it to him until it grows again." (16) If one wounded his neighbor they would say to him [the victim], "Give him a fee for bloodletting you." (17) He who crossed over with the ferry had to pay four *zuzim*, while he who crossed through the water had to pay eight. On one occasion, a certain porter happened to come there. Said they to him, "Give us four *zuzim* [for the use of the ferry]." But, protested he, "I crossed through the water!" "If so," said they, "you must give eight *zuzim* for passing through the water." He refused to give it, so they assaulted him. He went before the judge, who ordered, "Give them a fee for bloodletting and eight *zuzim* for crossing through the water." Now Eliezer, Abraham's servant, happened to be there, and was attacked. When he went before the judge, he said, "Give them a fee for bloodletting." Thereupon he took a stone and smote the judge. "What is this?" he exclaimed. He replied, "The fee that you owe me [for bloodletting], give to this man [who attacked me], while my money will remain in status quo."

(18) Now, they had beds upon which travelers slept. If he [the guest] was too long, they shortened him [by chopping off his feet]; if too short, they stretched him out.

Eliezer, Abraham's servant, happened to go there. Said they to him, "Arise and sleep on this bed!" He replied, "I have vowed since the day of my mother's death not to sleep in a bed."

(19) If a poor man happened to come there, every resident gave him a *dinar*, upon which he wrote his name, but no bread was given him. When he died, each came and took back his.

(20) They made this agreement among themselves: whoever invites a man [a stranger] to a feast shall be stripped of his garment. Now, a banquet was in progress, when Eliezer chanced there, but they gave him no bread. Wishing to dine, he went and sat down at the end of them all. Said they to him, "Who invited you here?" He replied to the one sitting near him, "You invited me." The latter said to himself, "Perhaps they will hear that I invited him, and strip me of my garments!" So he took up his raiment and fled without. Thus he [Eliezer] did to all, until they had all gone; whereupon he consumed the entire repast.

(20a) A certain maiden gave some bread to a poor man, [hiding it] in a pitcher. Once it became known, they daubed her with honey and placed her on the parapet of the wall, and the bees came and stung her. Thus it is written, "And the Lord said, 'The cry of Sodom and Gomorrah, it is great,'" whereon Rav Yehudah commented in Rav's name: On account of the maiden ["Riva"] (*Sanhedrin* 109a-b).

The examples cited in *Sanhedrin* 109a-b can be categorized as follows:

a) Violations of the seven Noachide commandments:

- sexual immorality (1);
- blasphemy (3);
- thievery (6, 6a, 7, 9, 10, 13, 13a);
- murder (indirect, 6, 10a, 18, 20a).

b) The Noachide code mandates that laws be established, which the residents of Sodom had. However, their laws were patently unfair, unethical and insensitive, represented poetically by the allegorical names of the four judges listed, "There were four judges in Sodom: Shakrai, Shakurai, Zayyafi, and Mazle Dina." According to the Soncino translation, "These are fictitious names meaning, Liar, Awful Liar, Forger, and Perverter of Justice." Their failure to write laws that were moral is evident in the following ways:

- A fatherless orphan is not entitled to property (7);
- Taking pledges from a widow even when the article taken significantly impacts on her ability to support herself (8);
- Illogical rules governing communal responsibilities (11);
- Unfair pricing for services rendered (12, 17);
- Improper adjudication for personal damages (14-16);

c) By far, the most concerted laws and policies satirized in *Sanhedrin* 109 are those maliciously designed to dissuade outsiders from benefitting from the abundance of resources present within these cities and environs. In addition to the statement in the Talmud to this effect, the Torah itself describes the beauty and attractions of Sodom: "And Lot lifted up his eyes, and beheld all the plain of the Jordan, that it was well-watered everywhere, before the Lord destroyed Sodom and Gomorrah, like the garden of the Lord, like the land of Egypt, as you go to Zoar" (Gen. 13:10). The following are laws that reject the idea of hospitality:

- The overall policy of dissuading visitors and guests (5);
- Torture in the guise of hospitality (18);
- While giving the impression of being charitable in the short run, the ultimate aim is to recover all that was invested via cruel treatment that ultimately kills the recipient (19);
- Punishments to whomever tried to surreptitiously support the indigent (who usually would be those who specifically came to town looking for support) (20, 20a).

d) An overall criminal attitude in all matters governed by law and rules:

- Premeditated sinfulness (4).

If we wish to corroborate R. Elazar's claim that extreme injustice was present in Sodom and Gomorrah, it is unclear that all of the things that the Talmud described were reflections of a lack of justice. Certainly, premeditated sinning in general, and specific violations of the Noahide commandments constituted terrible infractions that begged for divine punishment. And Sodom and Gomorrah's system of laws could be said to reflect a perversion of justice rather than its advancement and preservation. Unduly harsh laws and penalties justified the destruction of Sodom and Gomorrah in the spirit of *middah ke-neged middah*, "measure for measure," discussed above. Less clear, however, is whether the policies of eradicating charity and hospitality—while mean-spirited and miserly—should also be viewed as a type of lack of justice.

However, a case could be made that refusal to engage in charitable acts is unjust. Such an argument would support R. Elazar's contention in the Midrash. The Hebrew word for charity is *tzedakah*, a word derived from the root *tzedek*, which means "righteousness." *Tzedek* is definitely associated with justice in the Torah, as in the verses, "And I charged your judges at that time, saying: 'Hear the disputes between your brothers, and judge righteously [*tzedek*] between a man and his brother, and the stranger that is with him,'" (Deut. 1:16) and, "Justice, justice [*tzedek tzedek*] shall you pursue, that you may live, and inherit the land which the Lord your God gives you" (Deut. 16:20).

But the switch from *tzedek* to *tzedakah* transforms the concept from "righteousness" to what is typically understood as "charity." In the Bible the word *tzedakah* is paired with *mishpat* (justice), as in the verse:

> And David reigned over all Israel; and David executed justice and righteousness [*mishpat u-tzedakah*] unto all his people (2 Sam. 8:15).

The Talmud deliberately distinguishes between *tzedakah* and *mishpat* in at least one of its glosses[13] regarding the manner in which King David judged his people:

The Great Principle of the Torah

> In rendering legal judgment, David used to acquit the guiltless and condemn the guilty; but when he saw that the condemned man was poor, he helped him out of his own purse, thus executing judgment and charity, justice to the one by awarding him his due, and charity to the other by assisting him out of his own pocket. And therefore Scripture says, "David practiced justice and charity [*tzedakah*] towards all his people" (*Sanhedrin* 6b).

While it could be said that David helped poor litigants out of the goodness of his heart, one could alternatively say that he did so because of a sense of obligation, rather than as an exercise in optional kindness. Consider the Torah's description of a transaction between the rich and the poor:

> If there be among you a needy man, one of your brethren, within any of your gates, in your land which the Lord your God gives you, you shall not harden your heart, nor shut your hand from your needy brother; but you shall surely open your hand to him, and shall surely lend him sufficient for his need regarding what he wants. Beware that there be not a base thought in your heart, saying: "The seventh year, the year of release, is at hand"; and your eye be evil against your needy brother, and you give him nothing; and he cry unto the Lord against you, and it be a sin for you. You shall surely give him, and your heart shall not be grieved when you give to him; because for this thing the Lord your God will bless you in all your work, and in all that you put your hand towards (Deut. 15:7-10).

This passage contains negative as well as positive commandments. Such language suggests that to deny someone aid on principle, as the residents of Sodom and Gomorrah did, is considered a violation of Torah law. This includes all forms of support, such as withholding food, as well the unwillingness to offer financial assistance in the form of loans and gifts. When Sodom declared war on acts of *chesed*, it was not mere idiosyncrasy, but resulting from an extreme lack of justice in their society. In other words, from the Jewish perspective, giving charity is a legal obligation, and failure to engage in such activities is an absence of justice.

Verse 10 in the passage above reads: "...Because that for this thing the Lord your God will bless you in all your work, and in all that you put your hand into." The simple meaning is that someone who engages in acts of charity will be rewarded for the performance of that commandment. A second explanation is that God only blesses people with material wealth so they can put the money to work by performing commandments such as charity. Consequently, collectively instituting laws and policies intended to dissuade charitable activity is as much of an injustice—in accordance with the law's spirit if not its letter—as ignoring the Noachide laws or creating a law system that is unfair and immoral. Such an approach would support the understanding that every element in *Sanhedrin* 109a-b, including (or especially) the rejection of charitable behavior, as a reason Sodom and Gomorrah were the paradigm of injustice, and therefore it was inevitable that God would destroy such a malicious pair of cities.

Injustice in Jerusalem
R. Elazar says that Jerusalem, like Sodom, was destroyed because it was an unjust city. But while Sodom and Gomorrah were

destroyed by fire and brimstone, Jerusalem was besieged by foreign armies (2 Kings 25).[14]

But while the Talmud clearly corroborates R. Elazar's contention that injustice was rampant in Sodom and Gomorrah, there are numerous theories for the downfall of Jerusalem. The most famous passage about the destruction of Jerusalem and the two Temples is as follows:

> Why was the First Temple destroyed? Because of three things which prevailed there: idolatry, sexual immorality, bloodshed....[15] But why was the Second Temple destroyed, seeing that in its time they were occupying themselves with Torah, the commandments, and the practice of charity? Because therein prevailed hatred without cause. That teaches you that groundless hatred is considered as of equal gravity with the three sins of idolatry, immorality, and bloodshed together (*Yoma* 9b).

The First Temple was destroyed because of immorality, which closely parallels the wicked practices of Sodom and Gomorrah. However the Second Temple was destroyed because of *sinat chinam*—hatred without cause. However, "hatred without cause"[16] appears to be a much more subtle form of transgression than outright injustice. Most people would agree that harboring hatred without cause is not a good trait. However there is not a one-to-one correlation between how someone feels and how that person behaves. As long as the person behaves properly, then the sin of hatred should be between man and God, not between man and man. His hatred might cause him not to feel unified with the rest of the community, but does that constitute a lack of justice in the way R. Elazar was suggesting?

Furthermore, there are many other suggestions as to why Jerusalem was destroyed:

Abaye said: Jerusalem was destroyed only because the Sabbath was desecrated therein....

R. Abbahu said: Jerusalem was destroyed only because the reading of the Shema morning and evening was neglected....

R. Hamnuna said: Jerusalem was destroyed only because they neglected [the education of] school children....

Ulla said: Jerusalem was destroyed only because they [its inhabitants] were not ashamed of each other....

R. Yitzchak said: Jerusalem was destroyed only because the small and the great were made equal[17]....

R. Amram son of R. Shimon b. Abba said in R. Shimon b. Abba's name in R. Chanina's name: Jerusalem was destroyed only because they did not rebuke each other....

Rav Yehudah said: Jerusalem was destroyed only because scholars were despised therein....

Rava said: Jerusalem was destroyed only because men of faith ceased therein... (*Shabbat* 119b).

For Rav Yehudah said in Rav's name: What is meant by, "Who is the wise man, that he may understand this [... for what is the land destroyed]" (Jer. 9:11)? Now, this question was put to the Sages, Prophets, and ministering angels, but they could not answer it, until the Almighty Himself did so, as it is written, "And the Lord said: 'Because they have forsaken My Law which I set before them, and have not obeyed My voice, neither walked therein'" (v. 10). But is not "have not obeyed My voice" identical with "neither walked therein"? Rav Yehudah said in Rav's name: They did not first recite a benediction over the Torah (*Nedarim* 81a).

R. Yochanan said: "Jerusalem was destroyed only because they gave judgments therein in accordance with biblical law." Were they then to have judged in accordance with untrained arbitrators? — But say thus: "Because they based their judgments [strictly] upon biblical law, and did not go beyond the requirements of the law" (*Bava Metzia* 30b).

Some of these shortcomings, like failure to believe in God, recite Shema, or observe Shabbat, cannot be considered unjust in the conventional sense of the term. They might demonstrate a lack of gratitude for all that God has done for the Jews, but they do not reflect the idea that justice is absent in such a society. Lack of shame and failure to rebuke reflect indifference to the spiritual wellbeing of oneself and one's neighbors, but again, cannot be classified as injustice. Failure to educate children, refusal to critique one another's behavior, and the despising of scholars, might contribute to a society's inability to overcome its shortcomings, but once again do not necessarily qualify as examples of injustice. And as for observing biblical law without wavering, this appears to set a standard higher than conventional justice, and demands one to strive to go above and beyond what the letter of the law requires. Though this is a lofty goal, R. Yochanan said it was this failure that resulted in Jerusalem's destruction.

The Manifold Reasons for Jerusalem's Destruction

Rabbi Jacob Reischer (1661-1733), in his commentary *Iyun Yaakov*,[18] questions whether any of these explanations for the destruction of Jerusalem is objective, even the opinion of R. Elazar:

> And each one gives his rebuke in accordance with the needs of his generation which also was deemed guilty of the same transgression.

According to the view of the *Iyun Yaakov*, while all these iniquities may have been present when Jerusalem was destroyed, each rabbinic commentator had his eye upon what he thought was a blatant shortcoming within his own community. By associating the sin with Jerusalem's ruin, each rabbi highlighted these objectionable practices for the community which he was leading. The fate of Jerusalem may then have been utilized as a paradigm to get their communities to fulfill the commandments and develop proper traits more carefully, with the specific reasons being ahistorical.

Alternatively, it is possible that all of these flaws were present in Jerusalem when it was destroyed. In this case, the diversity of opinions is explained not by their lack of historical justification, but by each rabbi's personal outlook on the world. Different leaders, based on their own outlooks on the world and their own psychological compositions, chose to lay the emphasis in different places. As opposed to the *Iyun Yaakov* who said the historical accuracy is not important, this explanation would say all explanations are historically accurate, but psychologically each person chose to highlight a different shortcoming.

A third reading could say that the different arguments are a sort of triage. Each sin may have been present in Jerusalem (as opposed to *Iyun Yaakov* who argues the historicity is irrelevant), but different rabbis wanted to rebuke their communities for different failures, and their teachings are strategic calculations about which sins could not be tolerated in their own times, and so they used the model of Jerusalem's destruction to instruct their own communities.

However, of all the sins mentioned in the Talmud, aside from the three cardinal transgressions associated with the destruction of the First Temple, it is safe to say that R. Elazar's interpretation that a dearth of justice led to Jerusalem's destruction, is the most basic and obvious.

Equating Jerusalem with Sodom and Gomorrah
If we accept R. Elazar's view to the exclusion of the other suggestions, the prophet's equation of Jerusalem with Sodom and Gomorrah is fitting but also truly disconcerting:

> The vision of Isaiah the son of Amoz, which he saw concerning Judah and *Jerusalem*.... Had it not been that the Lord of hosts had left to us a very small remnant, we should have been as Sodom, we should have been like unto Gomorrah. Hear the word of the Lord, rulers of Sodom; give ear unto the law of our God, people of Gomorrah (Isa. 1:1, 9-10).

In v. 9, Isaiah suggests that Jerusalem should have suffered the same fate as Sodom and Gomorrah; v. 10 likens both the rulers and the inhabitants of these cities to one another. When we note what happened to Sodom and Gomorrah, it should not be difficult to understand, from R. Elazar's point of view, why Jerusalem suffered a parallel fate. While God promised never again to bring a flood that would wipe out all of creation, there would still be divine punishments against nations, cities, and individual people who have sinned. Whereas the Jewish individual reading the Bible may not immediately identify with Sodom and Gomorrah as relevant, the same cannot be said about the Jewish population of Jerusalem and the tragic events surrounding that city. Perhaps on the fast days commemorating the sieges and destruction of Jerusalem and the Temple, R. Elazar would single out the issue of *mishpat* in his exhortations to his community, and how important it is to behave in accordance with this basic Jewish value in order to avoid future terrible punishments.

Judah and Tamar

R. Elazar's third argument for the centrality of justice is from Judah and Tamar, and to me this seems the most powerful piece of his presentation. When Judah vindicated Tamar, despite the grievous cost to his own reputation, that is the greatest personification of justice.

The climax of the biblical account involving Judah and Tamar occurs when Tamar, who was pregnant, appears before her father-in-law, Judah. According to the rule of levirate marriage,[19] since Tamar had previously been married to first Er and then Onan,[20] both sons of Judah, she was required to wait for Shelah, Judah's third son, rather than marrying someone outside of Judah's immediate family.[21] When she became pregnant, that indicated she had violated the provisions of levirate marriage. In response Tamar produced indisputable evidence, identifiable only to Judah himself, that he had been intimate with her, and therefore was likely the father of her child. R. Elazar adds the additional factor that all of this was taking place in the presence of the rest of Judah's family. According to R. Elazar his grandfather Isaac, his father Jacob, and his brothers all aggressively defended Judah from Tamar's embarrassing accusation. Perhaps Tamar lacked standing to contradict this distinguished group of men, and therefore R. Elazar offers a parable, depicting Tamar like an orphan. By singling out the most defenseless members of a society—widows, orphans, strangers, and converts—for special protection, the Bible provides a clear way to measure the extent to which justice is present in a community or nation.[22] One would expect that if Judah was sitting in judgment of Tamar, he would not judge fairly, since an honest verdict would result in his own humiliation. The most likely result was that Tamar would have been condemned to death for her crimes. R. Elazar therefore emphasizes how Judah defied convention, judged in Tamar's favor, and came to embody Judaism's model of the ideal judge.

Of R. Elazar's three proofs, the argument from Judah and Tamar is most relatable and human,[23] in contrast with the first two proofs, which are more abstract. Many of the laws in *Parashat Mishpatim* are more abstruse than practical to most people. They demonstrate that society's laws should be structured, but it is uncertain that they will shape an individual's perception of justice in a day-to-day sense. Descriptions of the perversities in Sodom and Gomorrah, as well as Jerusalem, can perhaps influence interpersonal behavior when one reflects on contemporary examples of inhumanity. But any lasting effects from such arguments are offset by the sense that these events happened so long ago that they cease to be relevant. However, when we consider the very specific human example of Judah, we can appreciate to a much greater extent the different tensions that present themselves in our lives. Recognizing how Judah behaved ethically will provide a model for how we can live up to the highest ideals of justice and fairness. This story, in my opinion, has the greatest potential to form a lasting impression upon even a modern reader.

Complex Questions of Justice

But even if the example of Judah is the most persuasive of R. Elazar's arguments, it is important to keep at least three things in mind regarding the value of justice and this specific proof.

Rabbi Jonathan Sacks, in a recent essay titled "The Heroism of Tamar,"[24] places the emphasis upon Tamar rather than Judah in his reading of this biblical story:

> ... the real hero of the story was Tamar. She had taken an immense risk by becoming pregnant. Indeed she was almost killed for it. She had done so for a noble reason: to ensure that the name of her late husband was perpetuated. But she took no less care to avoid Judah being put to shame. Only he and she knew what had happened. Judah could acknowledge his error without loss of face. It was from this episode that the sages derived the rule… Rather risk being thrown into a fiery furnace than shame someone else in public.

Because of her personal resolve and humility, Tamar could be viewed as profoundly assisting Judah in making a clear choice. Tamar's heroic silence enabled her father-in-law to deliberate about how to respond, and ultimately judge fairly. Things might have been different if Tamar had openly accused Judah of indiscretion. At the very least, it would have been harder for

Judah to evaluate what was the right thing to do. Judah probably would have responded defensively, and concluded that that it was more important to publicly preserve his honor than to admit that he fathered Tamar's child. Such a response might have meant God would have selected someone else to be the progenitor of Jewish kings.

In addition, this story suggests that there are many determining factors that influence a person's ability or willingness to act justly. The question becomes: to what extent did Tamar's silence contribute to Judah's decision to act justly? If due to extreme circumstances, someone fails to act in accordance with their own values, that could indicate that these values are only surface-level, and not deeply rooted in the person's soul. On the other hand, it could be that all values are dependent on the specific situation, and it's impossible that facts and circumstances will not impact behavior, even if someone is a truly committed and moral individual. It is possible that even in the best-case scenario, ideal justice will inevitably be subject to the physical situation in which the individual finds himself.

However, someone who champions justice as the highest value might become overly judgmental in dealing with others. On the one hand, justice is basic and crucial for the prolonged viability of the society. But this realization does not mean that a person who is not a judge should have unrealistically strict expectations for their own behavior or the behavior of others. Exclusive devotion to *middat ha-din* (the attribute of justice) may mean we never give people the benefit of the doubt, and we may fail to live up to the lesson of judging everyone favorably (*Avot* 1:6; 6:5-6). It is true that there is an idea to emulate God, and we discussed *imitatio dei* in earlier chapters. And God is frequently described as both forgiving but also strict with justice (see, e.g., Exod. 34:6-7). However, we are told that if we are forgiving to those around us, then God will take a merciful approach with us as well:

> Rava said: He who forgoes his right [to exact punishment] is forgiven all his iniquities, as it says, "Forgiving iniquity and passing by transgression" (Micah 7:18). Who is forgiven iniquity? One who passes by transgression [against himself] (*Rosh Hashanah* 17a).

The tension between justice and compassion is even played out from a legal perspective in the Talmud's debate whether or not compromise (*rachamim*) is to be preferred to the strict maintenance of justice:

> R. Eliezer the son of R. Yosi the Galilean says: "It is forbidden to arbitrate [*botze'a*] in a settlement, and he who arbitrates thus offends, and whoever praises such an arbitrator condemns the Lord, for it is written, 'He that blesses an arbiter [*botze'a*], condemns the Lord' (Ps. 10:3). But let the law cut through the mountain, for it is written, 'For the judgment is God's' (Deut. 1:17). And so Moses' motto was: 'Let the law cut through the mountain.' Aaron, however, loved peace and pursued peace and made peace between man and man, as it is written, 'The law of truth was in his mouth, unrighteousness was not found in his lips, he walked with Me in peace and uprightness and did turn many away from iniquity'"(Malachi 2:6).
>
> R. Yehoshua b. Korcha says: "Settlement by arbitration is a meritorious act, for it is written, 'Execute the judgment of truth and peace in your gates'[25] (Zechariah 8:16). Surely

where there is strict justice there is no peace, and where there is peace, there is no strict justice! But what is that kind of justice with which peace abides? — We must say: Arbitration" (*Sanhedrin* 6b).

Although a fair trial is the cornerstone of civilized society, and even included in the Noachide law, the participants in the trial will have emotional responses to the outcome. It is spiritually important for the judge and litigant to be sensitive to the process in which they are involved. Therefore even if one litigant is clearly right in the eyes of the law, is declaring so necessarily the highest value? Is it possible that compromise is to be preferred, especially if it leads to increased harmony, peace, and even repentance by the wrongdoer? This is the dispute between R. Eliezer and R. Yehoshua ben Korcha.

One response to this dilemma is to hold oneself to a high standard while being more forgiving of those around us. In other words, we should judge ourselves with *middat ha-din*—the attribute of strict justice. In *Pirkei Avot*, Shammai taught, "Establish times for Torah study; say little but do much; and receive every person with a goodly countenance" (*Avot* 1:15). The first two statements are inwardly directed and set a personal standard of behavior. The third statement means that we should accept everybody with warmth and not take notice of their flaws, even if they don't study Torah regularly or engage in acts of kindness.

When we deal with others, both individually and collectively, we should apply *middat ha-rachamim* as kindly and charitably as possible. This is not only an interpersonal guidance, but a theological realization as well. Theologically, only God is considered the *Bochein ha-Levavot* (the One who inspects hearts). Perhaps if we recognize how difficult it is to understand the intentions and motivations of others, we can be more forgiving of those around us. In a courtroom setting, we require a very high standard of evidence to extract compensation for damages and especially for corporal punishment. Even in court, these elements must be proven, and we generally are not permitted to take these matters into our own hands (see, e.g., *Bava Kamma* 27b). Perhaps this recognition can help us temper our instinct to clamor for justice in personal matters as well.

Even with regard to one's own actions, Jewish law says that a person cannot incriminate himself (*ein adam meisim atzmo rasha*), which throws self-perception into question. If someone cannot always understand his own actions, how will he properly understand the acts of others? It is true that there are cases where people are not guilty in an earthly court but are held liable in the court of heaven (*patur be-dinei adam ve-chayav be-dinai shamayim*).[26] Many actions are beyond human capabilities to judge adequately and are therefore out of our hands. At the same time, if we believe we have committed an action for which we could technically evade punishment, we should nonetheless make compensation to those we have injured and ask their forgiveness.

A third concern with adherence to strict justice comes from R. Yochanan, who said that Jerusalem was destroyed "because they based their judgments on [strict] biblical law and did not go beyond the requirements of the law" (*Bava Metzia* 30b). R. Yochanan's comment seems counterintuitive in light of Isaiah's statement that Jerusalem was destroyed because of a lack of justice. R. Elazar highlighted that Isaiah condemned the lack of justice in Israel in his time. R. Yochanan, in contradistinction to R. Elazar, insists that adhering to the letter of the law, which is what Isaiah championed, could also lead to disaster!

The Great Principle of the Torah

According to the Talmud, the Second Temple was destroyed because of causeless hatred. Logically, this implies that the people must have behaved in a just way, since it would make no sense for the Sages to put forth such a subtle sin as *sinat chinam* if they could have accused them of greater crimes and outright injustice. In contrast to the sins that caused the demise of the First Temple, the Jews of the Second Temple studied Torah, observed the commandments, and gave charity willingly. The Talmud accuses that generation of causeless hatred, which means that the sins they committed were within themselves, and it is unlikely that they committed sins outwardly if they were only criticized for committing sins inwardly.

Several talmudic commentaries suggest that prior to the fall of Jerusalem, the judges and litigants did not engage in criminal behavior, but they took an improper attitude when participating in the legal process. Rabbi Abraham Chaim ben R. Naftali Tzvi Hirsch Shor, in his commentary on the Talmud called *Torat Chaim*, wrote:

> Since the judges do not have the authority to compel litigants to pursue compromise rather than go to trial, if the litigants each insist that the law be applied in its strictest sense, this is another manifestation of "hatred without cause" that the Talmud in *Yoma* 9b has cited as the reason for the destruction of the Second Temple. Consequently the Talmud's comment has to do with the litigants rather than the conduct of the judges (s.v. *ella eima she-he'emidu*).

The *Daf al Daf*[27] gives the following similar explanation, which has been paraphrased:

This is an interpretation that is reflected in the verse, "Justice, justice shall you pursue, that you may live, and inherit the land which the Lord your God gives you" (Deut. 16:20). Even if the judge is adjured to judge fairly and righteously according to the law, i.e., "You shall do no unrighteousness in judgment; you shall not favor the person of the poor, nor favor the person of the mighty; but in righteousness shall you judge your neighbor" (Lev. 19:15), the litigants should also pursue a path of "going beyond the letter of the law." Once the idea of inheriting the land of Israel is introduced in Deut. 16:20, this can be connected to Abraham, who was the initial recipient of the land, and about whom is stated, "For I have known him, to the end that he may command his children and his household after him, that they may keep the ways of the Lord, to do righteousness and justice; to the end that the Lord may bring upon Abraham that which He had spoken of him" (Gen. 18:19) — "way of the Lord" representing going beyond the letter of the law (see s.v. *be-Panim Yafot, Parashat Shoftim*).

Another commentary applies R. Yochanan's observation about going beyond the letter of the law to the story of Kamtza and Bar Kamtza, the famous event that indirectly caused the downfall of the Temple. This commentary focuses on the fact that even though there were many great rabbis in attendance at the party, none of them protested the humiliation Bar Kamtza would feel if he was ejected. The *Daf al Daf* writes:

The commentator bases himself on an interpretation by R. Yaakov Vermiz, cited by the *Chatam Sofer* [1762-1839] on *Gittin* 55b, the story of Kamtza and Bar Kamtza. R. Yaakov explains that when it states in *Pesachim* 113b that when one sees another doing something objectionable, while it is not permissible to testify against him as a single witness, nevertheless it is a commandment to hate him [i.e., justified hatred]. Tosafot writes that even if it is a commandment to hate such a person, one should not publicly demonstrate such hatred, as an act of going beyond the letter of the law. By implication, to publicly show disapproval of what is taking place in such an instance would be in accordance with the law, something ideally to be transcended. Turning to the well-known discussion of the incident referred to as "Kamtza and Bar Kamtza," when the scholars witnessed Bar Kamtza's humiliation by his enemy, while they did nothing to further humble the individual—thereby acting above and beyond the letter of the law [*lifnim mi-shurat ha-din*]—they also did not require the others present at the party to do the same, because the actions of the others were according to the law (s.v. *matzinu shnei ma'amarei Chazal*).

In contrast to the Rabbis who are criticized in the incident of Kamtza and Bar Kamtza, the Talmud contains a narrative illustrating how one Rabbi meticulously went beyond the letter of the law to stand up for what he regarded to be the proper treatment of another:

Shimon ben Shetach [supported himself by] producing linen fabric. His students said to him, "Rabbi! This is beneath your dignity. We will purchase for you a donkey and you will not need to further do this work." They went and bought for him a donkey from a Syrian. A jewel [was found] to be attached to its neck. They came to him and said, "You will no longer have to work at all!" He said to them, "Why?" They said to him, "We bought a donkey from a Syrian and a jewel was hung around its neck." He said to them, "Did the seller know this?" They said to him, "No." He said to them, "We have to go and return it."

[They answered:] "Didn't R. Huna Bibi bar Gozlon in the name of R. HaTivon in the presence of Rebbe say: Even according to the view that stealing from a non-Jew is prohibited, everyone agrees that if he errs [in valuation] that it is permitted to keep it." [He said to them:] "What do you think—Shimon ben Shetach is a barbarian?" R. Shimon ben Shetach was more desirous of [a non-Jew declaring] "Let the name of the God of the Jews be blessed" than any sort of this-worldly reward (Jerusalem Talmud *Bava Metzia* 2:5).

By implication, R. Yochanan implies that the majority of the society took the position of R. Shimon ben Shetach's students rather than that of their teacher, standing behind justice (*mishpat*) rather than going above and beyond the letter of the law (*lifnim mi-shurat ha-din*).

Consequently, while devotion to justice is one of the meta-principles of Judaism, it appears to be subject to more reservations than any of the ones discussed in previous chapters. Based on these stories, one cannot indiscriminately advocate for the pursuit of justice, without weighing in other values and variables. As Rabbi

Joseph Soloveitchik has been attributed as saying, "*Halakhah* is the basement, not the penthouse."[28] As the obligation to go beyond the letter of the law becomes more widely accepted, paradoxically it is transformed from an ideal into the law itself. Perhaps *lifnim mi-shurat ha-din* becomes *din*.

Implications for Contemporary Jews

The creation of a just society, with all of its citizens devoted to doing the right thing, certainly serves as a meta-principle for Judaism. The Bible posits that God wished that all of mankind would adhere to the standard of justice, but after two successive failures—Noah's flood and the Tower of Babel—a single people, beginning with Abraham, was chosen to serve as a light unto the nations. The vagaries of human history have resulted in repeated persecutions of this people, at times causing the nation of Israel to withdraw from the world scene in order to collect itself and salve its wounds. But Israel has always returned to contribute to civilization by means of extraordinary individuals, significant communities, and now a political state that takes its rightful place among the nations of the world. Jewish history would contend that the justification for this people's continued existence over the course of history is to serve in an exemplary capacity for all of the best human virtues, and to have justice, one of the meta-principles, be a key component of the Jewish mission. Consequently, all Jews who consider themselves beholden to this tradition are called upon to strive to assure that the families, organizations, communities, societies, and the world in which they participate are deeply influenced by principles of fairness and justice. One motivation to dedicate ourselves to the principle of justice could stem from Jews having been extensively persecuted, therefore enabling them to truly empathize, as Hillel taught in Chapter 1. However, it should be clear that looking upon justice as an ideal notion, independent of our own tragic history, seems to me to be an important value in its own right. Although the interests of justice sometimes frustrate the desire for personal comfort and life-long goals, Jewish tradition calls upon us to rise above self-interest in pursuit of true justice and righteousness.

As important as being committed to communal, national, and international justice might be, it is also crucial, in my opinion, that religious individuals hold themselves to high standards of justice and fairness in their personal lives as well. Whenever a religious figure publicly fails to adhere to these values, as occurred in the case that I referenced in the introduction to this book, humiliation comes not only to the perpetrators, but to the entire system. The entire religion becomes associated with, or even blamed for, the regrettable actions of even one person who acted immorally, and the people who practice that religion are forced to justify why they value a system that seems to permit others to act so despicably.

In response we must strive for the ideals of true justice by always pursuing what is proper, submitting disputes to fair evaluation by objective third parties, and then abiding by their conclusions without protest. This is how we make sure that we do not miss the point of R. Elazar's teaching. All too often, if a religion's leaders engage in questionable actions or render dubious decisions, the result is widespread cynicism and skepticism about the religion as a whole. In order to maintain the continuity of our tradition, this cynicism must be blunted, and the only way to do that is by holding everyone involved, leaders and followers alike, to the highest possible standards.

R. Sacks' insight into the story of Judah and Tamar is intriguing. To what extent can we as individuals not only push ourselves to act justly, but contribute to an environment where others can bring out the best in themselves? I realize that it can be overwhelming for us to always try to be fair in every circumstance; to help others not only by our personal examples, but in the manner in which we relate to others, is an even more daunting prospect, but one that is certainly worth pursuing.

Finally, any system that involves rules of behavior, like religion, provides a justification for some people to be judgmental and excessively critical. And even if we are more forgiving of others and hold ourselves to a scrupulous standard, that can engender a sense of superiority. However, the opposite is also true, where compassion can quickly turn into relativism, and we then might struggle to establish minimum standards of essential issues of Judaism, like Shabbat, *kashrut*, Jewish divorce, conversion, and other topics, even if they are controversial. While being committed to a strict sense of justice is clearly a high Jewish value, it is deeply challenging to avoid the concomitant pitfalls that such an outlook might naturally create. Of all of the values discussed in this book, maintaining a balanced sense of justice without losing one's capacity for tolerance and respect for others and otherness, is most challenging.

Endnotes

1. The Ten Commandments are recorded at Exod. 20:2-13. *Parashat Mishpatim*, which contains the Jewish civil law, is found immediately following, at Exod. 21:1-23:9. The assumption of this Midrash is that whatever immediately follows the Ten Commandments takes on some added significance. See Yitzchak Etshalom's essay, available at the time of this publication, at http://www.torah.org/advanced/mikra/5757/sh/dt.57.2.05.html. In fact some of the Ten Commandments can be seen as interpersonal laws. The third commandment is to not swear falsely, which applies to courtroom situations. And the second tablet contains nothing but criminal and civil laws: the prohibitions on murdering, committing adultery, stealing, bearing false witness, and coveting.

2. According to Jewish tradition, all people, Jews and non-Jews, are obligated to set up courts of justice. See *Sanhedrin* 56a.

3. All Jewish kings are to descend from the tribe of Judah, based on the verse that Jacob gave on his deathbed: "The scepter shall not depart from Judah, nor the ruler's staff from between his feet, as long as men come to Shiloh; and unto him shall the obedience of the peoples be" (Gen. 49:10). For this reason, the kingship of Saul, the first Jewish king, was inherently going to fail, since Saul belonged to the tribe of Benjamin.

4. See Gen. 38:24-6.

5. *Yoma* 86a.

6. At a recent conference under the auspices of the Center for Modern Torah Leadership, at one point discussion centered around the question whether religion and politics can be viewed as separate entities. While theoretically, religion should not be involved with objectives that motivate political activity, since many religions, including Judaism, are played out

in the public realm and involve many people, the practical reality in my experience is that the two are always inherently intertwined.

7. Rabbinic ordination originated when Moses appointed Joshua as his successor to lead the Jewish people into the land of Israel (see Num. 27:18, 23). One of the Roman initiatives to break the Jews' morale was to outlaw the official designation of new rabbinic leaders, a decree that was last defied by R. Yehudah ben Bava as recounted in the Talmud.

8. *Fate and Destiny* (translation of *Kol Dodi Dofek*), Ktav, Hoboken, NJ, 2000, pp. 7-8.

9. Rashi, quoting the primary opinion in *Midrash Aggada*, says it means "theft." Ibn Ezra means it means "all kinds of theft," meaning even oppression (stealing one's freedoms) and adultery (stealing one's spouse). According to *Midrash Aggada* 19, in a secondary interpretation, *chamas* refers to murder and sexual immorality. Chizkuni says it refers to murder, idolatry, and sexual immorality, the three cardinal sins of Judaism.

10. See, e.g., Isa. 2:2-4.

11. See, e.g., the litany of rebukes in Leviticus 26 and Deuteronomy 28.

12. We made a similar observation in Chapter 4, according to the apocryphal statement of R. Pappa: "This is what is meant when people say, 'A thief just before he breaks in calls out to God.'"

13. The Talmud offers two other interpretations of the verse. R. Yehoshua b. Korcha says that *tzedakah* and *mishpat* are inextricably linked, especially in the form of arbitration. And Rebbi said that justice means awarding the victorious party his due, and *tzedakah* means removing the stolen items from the thief's possession.

14. In rabbinic texts, this destruction is described in detail in *Gittin* 56a, and *Eikhah Rabbati, Petichtachot* 9.

15. These three sins are deemed so heinous that even if one would be threatened with losing his life, he was to refrain from transgressing them (*Sanhedrin* 74a). When the Talmud accuses people of voluntarily breaching these sins, it is a major condemnation.

16. In Chapter 2, we saw R. Akiva's opinion that the central principle of Judaism is "you shall love your neighbor as yourself." One might therefore think that Judaism never countenances hatred. However, the Talmud suggests that even God Himself hates certain classes of people: those who speak one thing with their mouths but have another thing in their hearts; those who have evidence relevant to a trial but do not come forward; one who testifies when there is no witness to corroborate his testimony (*Pesachim* 113b). This talmudic passage concludes that it is a duty to hate such people, based on the verse, "The fear of the Lord is hatred of evil" (Prov. 8:13).

17. Maharsha says this means there was an excess of flattery.

18. On *Ein Yaakov, Shabbat* 119b, s.v. *amar R. Abbahu*.

19. See Deut. 25:5-6.

20. Gen. 38:6-10.

21. It might appear anachronistic to speak of "Torah law" prior to Mt. Sinai. There is however a tradition that even before the Torah was given, many of its laws were already observed. See, e.g., Mishnah *Kiddushin* 4:14.

22. Some places where the widow, orphan, stranger, and convert are identified for special protections are Exod. 22:21, Deut. 10:10, and Deut. 24:17.

23. I have always felt that the reason why the Bible continues to be the greatest best-seller in history, as well as so influential as a cornerstone of morality and human civilization, is that however much social mores and values change, human nature has essentially remained the same. Therefore, when we study the people in the Bible, we are holding up a mirror to ourselves. The same dynamics that are recorded in the classical biblical stories play out again and again in our own lives. A similar reason is given for why Rembrandt painted many biblical scenes, some of them repeatedly—he was grappling with personal issues that he could contemplate and reflect upon by depicted the characters of the Bible. Peter Pitzele, a psychiatric social worker, describes how he uses psychodrama based on biblical scenes to help patients address their own issues. See his books *Our Fathers' Wells: A Personal Encounter with the Myths of Genesis* (HarperOne, San Francisco, 1995) and *Scripture Windows: Towards a Practice of Bibliodrama* (Torah Aura, Los Angeles, 1998).

This line of reasoning also becomes relevant to the long-standing dispute about whether we should view biblical characters like Abraham and Moses as exemplary but nonetheless flawed, or if we should assume their conduct is unimpeachable. One opinion in the Talmud says their behavior is beyond reproach, and should not be questioned even it seems suspicious (see *Shabbat* 55b-56b). Others, like Nachmanides and Abarbanel, say that even though these biblical figures should be revered, their failures or sins should not be justified, since even great individuals are still humans and cannot fully escape sinning (see Nachmanides on Gen. 12:10 and Abarbanel on 2 Sam. 12:13). When we realize that our biblical role models are nonetheless human, it makes them more relatable when we consider our own shortcomings, and it also teaches us that repentance and improvement are always possible.

24. As of the date of publication of this book, his essay is available at: http://israelseen.com/2014/12/12/jonathan-sacks-the-heroism-of-tamar/

25. See Chapter 5 for an alternate interpretation of this verse.

26. See, e.g., *Bava Kamma* 56a.

27. A series of books, essentially for those who study the *daf yomi* (daily folio), and includes notes and elucidations from the great sages of previous generations as well as modern ones, according to the order of the Talmud. The editors are R. David Avraham Mendelbaum, R. Yehoshua Lefkowitz, and R. Avraham Noach ha-Levi Klein (Bar Ilan CD ROM).

28. This is quoted in slightly different form in Walter Wurzberger's *The Ethics of Responsibility: Pluralistic Approaches to Covenantal Ethics*, p. 32, where he quotes Rabbi Soloveitchik as saying, "Halakhah is not a ceiling but a floor." Wurzberger himself writes, "I do not recall when I heard his comment by Rabbi Soloveitchik" (p. 121 n. 1).

Conclusion

After All is Said and Done, What is the Point?

Over the course of the preceding seven chapters, we have attempted to delineate a number of Jewish "meta-values," based upon traditional texts and advanced by various rabbinical personalities. Each of these values is informed by a powerful belief in a personal God. The thinkers advocating the values each believe that because man is created in God's image, he possesses the capacity to act in accordance with various Divine values and attributes.

However, when these values are taken as a whole, it becomes apparent that at least some, if not all, of them are antithetical to one another, not only from man's point of view, but even God's Himself. Respecting, feeling compassion for and even loving all people may clash with considerations arising from strict adherence to the perspective of all-encompassing justice. Choices may have to be made between man's single-mindedly serving God and dedicating time and effort towards relating constructively to other human beings. Observance of Jewish ritual practices and acceptance of traditional definitions of personal status could result in sacrificing the value of always being, as well as being perceived, as pleasant and accepting. Perhaps most obviously, the values of *rachamim* (mercy) on the one hand, and *din* (justice) on the other, while both by definition constitute basic components of the Nature of God, appear to have a more holistic than rational, logical relationship with one another. Granted that in the Talmud and Midrash, certain personalities may have been attracted to one value over another due to their personal makeup and experience; nevertheless, when we find ourselves confronted with all of the dimensions of this material, rather than simply choosing whichever approach is most consonant with our own sensibilities, we should strive to include as many of these values as we can in how we conduct our lives. While all of these dialectical antitheses contribute to how mysterious God and His ways are to finite man, if Jews are charged in the Torah to "walk in God's ways," they find themselves tasked with turning these multiple distinct values into a hierarchy of priorities which should ideally inform their choices and actions. How is one supposed to do this when the values themselves, taken as a whole, appear to be intrinsically contradictory?

Perhaps the best that man can hope for is that when possible, he should engage in reflection and deliberation—either within his own mind, or together with others whom he respects—prior to undertaking a particular course of action. Such a deliberation would lay out the possibilities for future action, including consideration of which of an array of values, even conflicting ones, could inform what one ultimately decides to do. A result of such a protocol is that man will become more introspective, and less and less of his behaviors will be mechanical and unthinking. Using the terminology of Rabbi Soloveitchik, man should transform himself from a non-confronted being, simply moving with the flow of life around him, to a confronted individual who, via grappling

The Great Principle of the Torah

with "meta-principles," recognizes his responsibilities, personal, familial, communal and existential, as he lives his life.

Furthermore, how to respond to situations, particularly if they are on-going and will be of significant duration, will inevitably entail numerous "re-visitations," not only involving reevaluating and understanding afresh the "facts on the ground," but also the factors, including informing meta-values, that went into the decisions made leading up to this point, so that some clarity can be achieved in the interests of being able to go forward.

A rabbinic statement that captures such an ideal process appears in the Talmud:

> Our Rabbis taught: For two and a half years Beit Shammai and Beit Hillel were in dispute, the former asserting that it were better for man not to have been created than to have been created, and the latter maintaining that it is better for man to have been created than not to have been created. They finally took a vote and decided that it were better for man not to have been created than to have been created, but now that he has been created, let him investigate his past deeds or, as others say, let him examine his future actions (*Eruvin* 13b).

I think that the two versions of what the Talmud recommends that a person do in order to live the good life, i.e., look at his past or make decisions about his future, are not mutually exclusive, but rather complementary. The Talmud contends that as far as an individual is concerned, what he has done in the past, and now plans to do going forward, should never be isolated from one another. All of one's actions are of a piece, reflective of the individual's priorities as well as his deeply held aspirations. Once fault is found with such aspirations and assumptions, only significant changes will guarantee not repeating past follies and disappointments. Awareness of and engagement in carrying out meta-values, as opposed to specific *mitzvot* alone, can combat the human tendency towards compartmentalization that results in inconsistency and even hypocrisy. Consequently, devoting attention to whether one's actions have and will reflect loving and caring about others, devotion to and belief in God, perpetrating good deeds and acts of kindness, compassion, and justice will hopefully result in improving one's ways.

Aldous Huxley famously said, "The only completely consistent people are the dead." Therefore it is to be expected that people not always carry out their responsibilities with perfect consistency. Ecclesiastes similarly implies: "For there is not a righteous man upon earth, that doeth good, and sinneth not" (Eccl. 7:20). However, the likelihood of inconsistency and *Chillul Hashem* increases exponentially when no attempts are made to identify what are the things that are truly important and what we should all strive to incorporate into our lives. Hopefully the seven preceding chapters can contribute to setting an agenda for significant reflection and introspection. While the development of adopting a reflective approach towards the desired mindsets and behaviors articulated by the various rabbinic authorities we have discussed is a lifelong process, it is clearly the "point" to which everyone should dedicate his best efforts.

Appendix

The Relationship Between *Ta'amei ha-Mitzvot* (the Reasons for Commandments) and "What's the Point?"

The underlying premise of asking the question "What's the Point?" of Judaism is that the "point" is rationally identifiable and susceptible to general human understanding. If the only valid meaning of living a Torah lifestyle is mystical or metaphysical, Jews would have no choice other than to resign themselves to following directives of sacred book learning and/or inherited traditions, without reflection or introspection about these directives' individual or collective meaning. But when it is posited that the commandments, individually as well as taken as a whole, are accessible to philosophical, theological, and ethical investigation, we find ourselves endowed with the legitimate right, and perhaps even obligation under the rubric of the mitzvah to study Torah, to scrutinize our tradition to the greatest extent possible.

The ultimate goal of such intellectual and spiritual study is to personalize our religious experience in a self-conscious manner

Appendix

well beyond simply doing things because we believe that God and His representatives, the scholars of the tradition, have mandated them. The Maharal of Prague has suggested that the word "*Torah*" is derived from the verb *le-horot*, "to teach." Advocates of pursuing *ta'amei ha-mitzvot* would insist that the Divine teaching that is achieved via Torah study is not only what and how to live, but also why we are doing the things that we are doing in the name of religion. We are attempting to augment an essentially pragmatic, action-centered system of Torah commandments with philosophical questing and personal engagement. Ultimately discovering a purpose that truly resonates with us for each mitzvah allows us to draw closer to God's expectations for us, and thereby justify the internalization of ideas like the meta-values that have been discussed in the preceding chapters.

Naturally, when one opens the Pandora's box of curiosity and investigation, and applies it to religious truths, certain dangers, which otherwise lie dormant, come to life. What will ultimately be the effect of attributing to a certain commandment, let alone an entire class of commandments, or the Torah as a whole, reasoning that can result in disaffection or fundamental disagreement with the mitzvah under consideration, which in turn could lead to non-compliance, and perhaps possibly turn into alienation from the Torah as a whole? One example of such thinking is embodied in the Talmud's presentation of an aspect of King Solomon subjecting commandments directed at Jewish kings to his superior intelligence (1 Kings 5:9). The Talmud teaches:

> Said R. Isaac: Why were the reasons for the commandments not revealed? Because in two verses the reasons [for two commandments] were revealed, and [as a result] the great [mind] of the world [i.e., Solomon] stumbled on them.

> It is written, "He should not be married to a great number of wives, in order that his heart will not be turned aside…" (Deut. 17:17). Said Solomon: "I will marry many wives and I will not be diverted." And it is written, "And it was when Solomon was elderly, his wives diverted his heart" (1 Kings 11:4).
>
> And it is written, "And only he should not possess too many horses so that he will not return the people to Egypt in order to obtain many horses…" (Deut. 17:16). And Solomon said, "I will own many horses and I will not return [the Jewish people to Egypt]." And it is written, "And a chariot from Egypt would go up and cost 600 pieces of silver, and a horse for 150 pieces of silver…" (1 Kings 10:29) (*Sanhedrin* 21b).

Since Solomon is depicted as relying on only himself, without consulting with others who may have been able to mitigate the conclusions that he arrived at, the king's personal pursuit of *ta'amei ha-mitzvot* was the apparent catalyst for significant transgressions on his part.

A more contemporary example would entail the manner in which women are likely to respond to a particular reason given for their being exempt from positive time-bound *mitzvot*:

> A man takes precedence over a woman in matters concerning the saving of a life and the restoration of lost property (i.e., if both a man and a woman are simultaneously in danger and both cannot be saved, or, similarly in the lost object of both a man and a woman

could potentially be returned but both cannot be the man and his property take precedence over a woman and hers)... (*Horayot* 13a).

R. Ovadiah Bartenura, in his commentary on this Mishnah, writes, "Because he is holier, as indicated by a man being obligated in all commandments while a woman is not obligated in positive time bound commandments."

No one can be particularly comfortable being told that they are less holy than the next individual, let alone an entire gender, and such explanations have led at least some women to conclude that Judaism does not respect them and therefore the observant life is not worthwhile. However, Rabbi Samson Raphael Hirsch provides a much more appropriate answer in our current climate. He argues that since women are intrinsically more conscious of time, they are not in need of the constant reminders constituted by *mitzvot aseh she-ha-zeman gerama*, a view that is more existential than other interpretations.

Having alternate explanations for this type of exemption readily available is important in our current climate of heightened awareness of egalitarianism and other external societal influences.

In a more positive vein, the Torah itself emphasizes how important it is to have level-appropriate answers at hand when asked about the meaning of the *mitzvot*, both specifically and in general, via a number of verses devoted to either responding to questions, or even initiating the religious education, of one's children:

26. it shall come to pass, *when your children shall say unto you*: "What mean ye by this service?" 27. That ye shall say:

"It is the sacrifice of the Lord's Passover, for that He passed over the houses of the children of Israel in Egypt, when He smote the Egyptians, and delivered our houses" (Exod. 12:26-27).

And you shall *tell your son* in that day, saying, "It is because of that which the Lord did for me when I came forth out of Egypt" (Exod. 13:8).

And it shall be *when your son asks you* in time to come, saying, "What is this?" that thou shalt say unto him: "By strength of hand the Lord brought us out from Egypt, from the house of bondage" (Exod. 13:14).

20. *When your son asks you* in time to come, saying: "What mean the testimonies, and the statutes, and the ordinances, which the Lord our God has commanded you?" 21. Then you shall say unto your son: "We were Pharaoh's bondmen in Egypt; and the Lord brought us out of Egypt with a mighty hand. 22. And the Lord showed signs and wonders, great and sore, upon Egypt, upon Pharaoh, and upon all his house, before our eyes. 23. And He brought us out from thence, that He might bring us in, to give us the land which He swore unto our fathers. 24. And the Lord commanded us to do all these statutes, to fear the Lord our God, for our good always, that He might preserve us alive, as it is at this day. 25. And it shall be righteousness unto us, if we observe to do all this commandment before the Lord our God, as He has commanded us" (Deut. 6:20-25).

Appendix

In none of these instances is the reason given that commandments are to be done simply because God has commanded us to do them. It would appear that it is assumed that this will simply not suffice in most cases. The first three sources above refer to Jewish history and our obligation to reciprocate for God's having saved us from servitude. The last source adds theological and spiritual dimensions, i.e., the basis for a Jewish presence in the land of Israel, fearing God is in man's best interests, compliance with *mitzvot* as an act of *tzedakah*, that could be said are intrinsic to the service of God. Intriguingly, we are not made privy as to how these archetypes of young learners responded to what their parent explained to them. Did they simply accept what they were told, or did they "push back" and raise objections to their parents' presentations? We can, however, well imagine that if such explanations did not elicit indications that the child understood, and commitment to a Jewish lifestyle could be expected, the parent would try alternate explanations that might better resonate with the questioner. Furthermore, an explanation that makes sense to a younger, more concrete thinker, definitely has to be revised as the individual matures, develops his ability to appreciate abstract concepts and grows in overall intellectual sophistication. Just as such a progression obviously pertains to an individual over the course of his lifetime, the same has been true for the Jewish people as a whole, with explanations that may have served well during the Middle Ages having to be revised, or even substituted for, in more modern times.

Maimonides, in the third section of the *Guide for the Perplexed*, posits that many commandments are intended to directly counter practices associated with idolatry. Since paganism is no longer widespread, at least in the Western world, alternative explanations will have to be sought in order to win and maintain "hearts and minds."

During my freshman year in college, R. Leonard Rosenfeld presented our class in Yeshiva University with a very cogent parable regarding understanding *ta'amei ha-mitzvot* which continues to inform my thinking to this day:

> Consider the elements that comprise the scientific method. (a) A natural phenomenon is observed, (b) a hypothesis is developed to account for the phenomenon and extend humanity's understanding of the laws of the universe, and (c) experiments are devised in order to test the verity of the hypothesis. In the event that the hypothesis is supported by the experiments, it can eventually be considered a demonstrable theory. If, however, the experiments disprove the hypothesis, another one will have to be developed and then tested.

The analogue in terms of *ta'amei ha-mitzvot* would be:

(A)	Phenomenon	Mitzvah
(B)	Hypothesis	*Ta'am*
(C)	Experiment	Analysis of primary sources and commentaries, and how they interact with other commandments

The relationship between the physical phenomena and the *mitzvot* is a powerful one. The physical universe exists independent of scientific understanding, and the obligation to perform *mitzvot* does not merely originate when someone achieves a personally satisfactory understanding of God's commandments. The only variable is the *ta'am*, which can be speculated about, investigated, and held up to scrutiny against other biblical and rabbinic sources, in pursuit of a deeper understanding of the *mitzvot*. To return to the metaphor of the scientific method, a physical phenomenon does not cease to exist when its causes cannot be documented, and the obligation to fulfill the commandments does not melt away just because we have not identified a suitable *ta'am*.

www.ingramcontent.com/pod-product-compliance
Lightning Source LLC
Chambersburg PA
CBHW030105240426
43661CB00001B/25